Pottery

art horizons

Pottery

Charles Lakofsky
Bowling Green University

WM. C. BROWN COMPANY PUBLISHERS
Dubuque, Iowa

ART HORIZONS SERIES

Consulting Editor

WILLARD F. WANKELMAN
Bowling Green University

A growing interest in art and art history is evident today in the United States and has created a need for a new approach in the formulation of classroom teaching materials.

The ART HORIZONS SERIES, designed for introductory courses in art appreciation and art history, transmits the excitement of the subject to the student seeking a liberal education. This series offers both the student and teacher flexibility of subject matter as well as authoritative writing in each topic area. Although the individual titles are self-contained, collectively they cover the major subjects usually discussed in an introductory course.

Copyright © 1968 by
Wm. C. Brown Company Publishers

Library of Congress Catalog Card Number: 68—14578

Printed in the United States of America

To KENNETH FRANCIS BATES,

for first and lasting insights into a world of beautiful things, beautifully done

acknowledgments

Few works, whatever their media, arise independently within the genius of an individual, but rather are a distillation of facts, of ideas and ideals, and of experiences which culminate in a personal outlook. For such, the writer is especially indebted to several teachers: Kenneth F. Bates and the late Charles F. Mosgo of the Cleveland Institute of Art; Clarence W. Merritt and the late Charles M. Harder of the State University of New York College of Ceramics at Alfred University, whose lecture notes and philosophies have been adapted or remembered in this work, as they have in many philosophies of teaching and of potting; and the late Carlton Atherton of The Ohio State University School of Art, for his discerning approach to ceramic enrichment.

The problems of assembling illustrative material were many, and thanks are afforded to Miss Lillian Kern, Registrar, The Cleveland Museum of Art; Mrs. Ruth Wilkins, Curator of Collections, Everson Museum of Art; Miss Vivian Scheidemantel, Associate Curator of Decorative Arts, and Anselmo Carini, Director of Publications, The Art Institute of Chicago; Mrs. Betty Toulouse, The School of American Research, Santa Fe, New Mexico; and the several commercial firms noted specifically along with the photographs they supplied. Gratitude is also expressed to many fellow potters, personal friends and some that are now felt to be friends, for the many photographs which they supplied, the number and quality of which made final selection a difficult but pleasant task.

Teaching colleagues at Bowling Green State University proved a willing source of assistance, and thanks are extended to Joseph Weber and Milford Lougheed for their advice on the sections concerning chemistry and geology, respectively. Special thanks are deserved by Mrs. Gwendolyn Lougheed of the English staff, who so patiently read and red-pencilled the manuscript; and by James Gordon of the School of Journalism for his discerning photography. All photographs, unless otherwise credited, are by Mr. Gordon.

introduction

Just as the common material known as clay bears the record of the action of untold ages of geologic time upon the crust of the earth, so the pottery which man of all times has formed from it is an index to his progress and to his creativity. For clay is the result of physical and chemical processes acting upon seemingly unchangeable rock, disintegrating it by the movement of glaciers or by freezing and thawing, dissolving and chemically altering and often moving it by water, to finally produce a material that is uniquely soft, workable, and receptive to the touch of the human hand. The pottery which has been produced from this material since neolithic times records indelibly the mechanical ingenuity and the cultural patterns of the peoples which produced it, a record so permanent and so revealing that few works on the general history of civilization or of art fail to cite pottery in their discussions of the beginnings of mankind.

It is fire, the ultimate tool of the potter, which gives to his works their final degree of hardness or permanence. This same fire, rather ironically, reverses the geologic metamorphosis of clay as it is changed within a relatively short period of time to a dense, often rocklike material similar to that which it was uncountable ages before the potter worked it, but this time bearing not the mark of geologic time but rather that of the ingenuity of man.

Few media at the command of any artist or craftsman are as innately versatile or ultimately permanent as are those of the potter. His raw materials can often be used unrefined as taken from their natural source, with perhaps only the removal of coarse impurities, or they can be refined and combined with other substances to achieve the most controlled of results. They can be formed into wares by the use of tools ranging from the simplest hand utensil to the complex automaton of the production line which requires the human factor only to watch it. Pottery remains the only significant art form in which the work can be executed by the hand alone, without pencil or brush, chisel or mallet. Clay can be shaped while in many stages of workability, from liquid to plastic to almost rigid, through the use of a wide variety of techniques to produce wares of great diversity in their forms. These wares can be enhanced from a palette rich in mineral and glaze colors, rich not only in color range but also in texture and surface quality. This palette can be varied by manipulation of its ingredients, by use of a myriad of decorative techniques, and by control of the firing process to give results ranging from a rather earthy and primitive quality to the most sophisticated and elegant of glaze colors and textures.

Once fired beyond the range of soft earthenware, ceramics achieve a permanence and hardness rivalled by no art medium other than the stone which they often so closely resemble. They are not subject to the damaging effects of moisture and rot as are canvas and wood, the chemical deterioration of paint and varnish, nor the oxidation or other chemical actions detrimental to certain metals. Conversely, wares which have not been fused to any great degree of glassiness, such as most primitive and earthenware vessels and those which are coated with glazes high in lead compounds, are subject to gradual deterioration because of structural weakness or chemical instability. Also inherent in pottery is a fragile quality, for strong though a piece may be, it is neither flexible as a fibre basket nor malleable as a metal vessel and is consequently subject to breakage. But though the pot be shattered, the potsherds can still tell a story!

And to survey, in a rather limited way, this story of the potter's art is the purpose of this short work. Many approaches might be taken, as suggested in the foregoing generalizations. A chronological, historical survey with consideration of the cultural and social factors contributing to the development of the art, an analysis of the design principles involved and their part in the esthetic statement, or an instructional manual in materials and technical methods are among the possibilities. Many books, however, are already available, excellent in their various and varied approaches to the techniques, history, and philosophy of the craft. It is the objective of this writer to consider pottery from the point of view of the nonpotter, who might seek insight into the magic of the art and its technicalities without being burdened or confused by objective factors at the expense of the creative. Such problems cannot be completely overlooked, however, for they comprise the majority of questions asked by the nonpotter.

Examples to illustrate particular technical or esthetic points have been selected from the wares of many times and cultures in the hope that they will not only make lucid a particular aspect, but also fall into a panorama depicting at once the timelessness, the universality, and some of the beauty of the potter's art.

contents

1. The Genus: Ceramics 1
   Ceramics • Clay products • Glass • Enamels

2. The Materials 4
   Inorganic and organic materials • Silicates • Feldspar •
   Clay • Primary clays • Secondary clays

3. The Types 13
   Derivation of names • Bodies • Earthenware • Stoneware •
   Porcelain • China • Bone china

4. The Fire 21
   Firing • Firing cycles • Kiln types • Kiln atmosphere •
   Firing controls • Pyrometric cones • Oxidation and reduction

5. The Forming 38
   Techniques • Slip casting • Coil building • The potter's
   wheel • Throwing • Jiggering • Slab building

6. The Forms 58
   Pottery forms • Cylindrical forms • Spherical forms •
   Faceted forms • Multiple forms • Figurative forms

7. The Enrichment 74
   Types of ornament • Plastic decoration • Slip decoration •
   Underglaze • Glazes • Glaze color • Majolica • Overglaze •
   Enamels • Luster • Metals

8. The Function 101

   Suggested Reading 105

   Glossary 107

   Index 111

xiii

The Genus: Ceramics

Figure 1. Medallion with Bust of Christ. Frankish Kingdom (second half of eighth century). Cloisonné enamel on copper, d. 1 15/16". The Cleveland Museum of Art, purchase from the J. H. Wade Fund.

Peculiar to man is his genius for fabricating raw materials into forms which satisfy his basic needs—either physical or emotional. One of the broad areas in which this capacity is manifest is that of "ceramics," a term derived from the Greek *keramikos* meaning potter's earth or anything made from it. The original term in itself is a fascinating one, for from it probably comes the Latin *cremo,* to burn or consume by fire, and hence the English *cremate.*

Although the term "ceramics" thus seems based on pottery, the ceramic world of the present day is much more comprehensive than the derivation of the word might imply, for it includes not only earthenware and pottery, but has been extended to include all products developed from earthy, inorganic, nonmetallic substances[1] treated to red heat or higher during their manufacture.[2] Included are all products which have clay as their basic material, such as pottery, bricks (other than cement

Figure 2. Double Balsamarium. Syria (third-fourth century A.D.). Olive green transparent glass with applied thread decoration. The Toledo Museum of Art, Curtis Collection, gift of Edward Drummond Libbey, 1923.

or concrete), clay drainage tile and sewer pipe, floor tiles (but not those of rubber or asphalt composition, which could hardly withstand red heat!), the porcelain section of spark plugs and electrical fixtures, and many others.

Also to be considered ceramic are those articles termed glass, which material falls within the above definition in that it is developed by melting silica in combination with agents called fluxes. Glass articles differ from clay products in that their structural material is melted before it is formed, given shape while in a relatively molten state, and becomes rigid during subsequent cooling. In contrast, clay products are shaped before their heat treatment.

The application of glassy or vitreous coatings to metal surfaces constitutes another category, that of enamels. Such coatings are to be found on many functional items used in contemporary living, including sinks, bathtubs, refrigerators, washers, driers, electrical fixtures, and gas station signs. Enamels are in themselves glasses, but rather than being independent structures as are glass products, these are fused to pre-formed metal. They are quite similar to pottery glazes in composition, differing in that they are applied to metal rather than to clay, and are usually prepared by melting the raw materials to a glass and grinding this glass into a powder before application to the metal where they receive a final remelting. (A distinct pottery application of enamels is discussed in the chapter on decorating techniques.) Excluded from the area of ceramics are the "baked-on" finishes which coat automobiles and their license plates, for they are neither glassy in composition nor fired to a red heat after application.

Enamels, however, are not relegated to the mundane kitchen, bathroom, or laundry, for they have long afforded a richness to the realm of decorative arts rivalled by few other media. Notable are the lovely religious works of the Gothic and Byzantine epochs, the French Limoges, Oriental cloisonné, and the contemporary use of enamels ranging from large architectural applications to some of infinite delicacy on jewelry and other small treasures.

Such works are perhaps far removed from the scope of pottery, but they seem worthy of mention because they indicate the complexity of the ceramic world of which pots are a part, and the breadth of that world which ranges from the most lowly to the most exquisite.

FOOTNOTES

[1]Many of the elements important in ceramics are, in their pure state, metals such as iron, calcium, and sodium. When used, however, they are in combination with other elements in compounds such as oxides and carbonates, and in their fired state are considered oxides. Hence, they are not metals as such. Exceptions are the gold and platinum used in decoration, and the minute layers of iridescent metal known as lusters.

[2]The lowest visible red heat is in the range of 1000 degrees Fahrenheit.

2

The Materials

Figure 3. Deposit of secondary clay remaining in the bottom of a mud puddle after evaporation of water. This clay, gray-green in color as found, fired to a typical flowerpot orange.

Although the raw materials of the potter are many and varied, they fall within a few general categories. Classification can be made according to sources, physical and chemical types, working properties, and the effect in the final functional and esthetic statement of the fired ware. The materials may be used crude and unrefined in their natural state as they have been in the wares of many primitives; they may be treated to remove impurities as have been the relatively pure kaolins and other clays available on the present-day market; or they may be chemically prepared as are the precipitated or otherwise altered compounds which are far from the state in which they were removed from their parent earth. Typical of the latter are the rather pure metallic compounds used as coloring agents in glazes.

Whether crude or refined, all ceramic materials hold several factors in common: they have the earth as their source, are inorganic,[1] and they must be able to withstand the elevated temperatures of firing without vaporizing. This last property, however, is relative to the degree of temperature to which the material is subjected. Some compounds are quite stable within certain temperature limits, such as those containing lead, and may be used at the relatively low earthenware range but would volatilize if fired at the higher range of stoneware and porcelain. Such volatilization is not always objectionable, for it is exploited in salt glazing and in certain glazes colored by transmutation.

Just as the earth is the prime source of ceramic raw materials, those materials which are the most important in ceramics hold one substance in common with the earth, silica. This oxide is a chemical combination of the two most abundant elements in the crust of this planet, oxygen and silicon, and might well be termed the backbone of the earth, for approximately 60 per cent of its crust consists of this oxide, whether in the pure silicates such as quartz or combined within minerals or aggregates as in feldspar and granite. Silica also might well be called the backbone of ceramics, for it is a certainty that without silica, the world, if it were here, would be without ceramics. It is the primary constituent in the minerals of the broad feldspathic group, so important as fluxes or glass-formers in pottery bodies and glazes and as the parent rock of the materials called clays. Silica imparts hardness to pottery bodies, glassiness to glazes, often surface texture to bricks, and even to a certain extent imparts to kilns their capacity to withstand the heat to which their contents are subjected.

With silicon heading the list of important elements, this list could be extended to include a great number of the one hundred-odd elements which have been identified. It is of interest that such elements, usually in combination with oxygen, are of ceramic importance in almost the sequence of their relative occurrence in the earth's crust. Following the 60 per cent of silica in that crust is alumina, the oxide of aluminum, which totals about 15 per cent and is a constituent of two most important ceramic materials, feldspar and clay. Next in abundance is iron, which gives to so many clays their characteristic tan or red tonality and is the most versatile and probably the most frequently used of all glaze coloring agents (in its red and black oxide, hydroxide, or carbonate forms it is also largely responsible for the color of the earth itself). Magnesium, calcium or lime, sodium, and potassium follow in abundance and importance. They are the principal fluxing agents in glasses, glazes, and clay bodies.

Whatever the source and composition of the potter's materials, however, his primary one is of course the clay from which he fabricates his wares. Clays are among the most abundant materials to be found and may be considered a curse or a means of potential beauty or utility. A deposit of the sticky stuff holds little appeal for the operator of a bulldozer who must fight its rubbery mass to excavate a roadbed or a building site, but it might suggest far more to a potter who fondles an excavated handful and envisions what it might become on his wheel and in his kiln. Its red muckiness might be cursed by an eager gardener who sinks his spade into it in the wet days of early spring, looking ahead to the flowers he might evoke from it were it only a little less sticky (peonies, it is claimed, do rather well in heavy clay loams); the same material might portend to the potter rich red earthenware pots or deep brown slip glazes—pots meant to hold and enhance the flowers envisioned by the impatient gardener.

This clay substance, chemically and geologically belonging to a broad group of minerals encompassing the hydrous silicates of alumina, is found world-wide, with considerable variation in composition and in working and fired properties. Its basic characteristics, which are its plasticity or workability when mixed with water, its capacity to be shaped and to retain that shape upon drying, and its fusion to some degree of glassiness when subjected to red heat or higher, have led it to be shaped by civilizations of all places and of all times since the neolithic age. The most important mineral present in clays is kaolinite,[2] and although deposits of pure kaolinite are unknown, white-burning China clays or kaolins are quite high in it, and all clays are mixtures of it in combination with other clay minerals or metallic oxides or hydroxides.

Where did this abundant clay come from? Its story can be integrated with that of the earth, for clay is evidence of the constant change which has been taking place on the crust of this planet since its genesis. Although there are many theories concerning the earth's origin, it is generally accepted that at one time it was molten, and as it cooled and subsequently solidified, at least at its surface, materials known as minerals crystallized out of the molten magma. Kaolinite, however, was not among the progeny of this prolific mother magma, for none was present as the mass solidified. It is, rather, the result of the decomposition of the most abundant mineral group of that mass, the feldspars. These comprise approximately 60 per cent of the earth's crust and are usually combined with other minerals in rocks such as granite or granodiorite.

The processes which alter the feldspathic rocks are many and complex but may be considered both physical and chemical weathering.

The physical processes simply reduce the particle size of minerals and ultimately result in a fine-grained mixture known as silt if no chemical phenomena are involved. Such physical weathering is the result of freezing and thawing, of abrasion during transportation by glacier and water, and even of seemingly insignificant yet persistent crushing by the powerful growth of plant roots as they seek their way among fractures or interstices of rocks.

Silt, however, is not clay, fine-grained though it may be. Clay is the result of chemical weathering, and the most important such process is kaolinization, which actually alters the crystalline and chemical structure of the parent minerals. Kaolinization is quite complex, but reduced to the simplest explanation, it may be thought of as the removing of the alkalis locked within the feldspar crystal and the recombining of the silica and alumina with the addition of water, resulting in the different crystalline mineral, kaolinite. This metamorphosis involves time, hardly measurable in days or years, taking place over the geologic eons about which geologists so love to rapture. Perhaps a sense of the time involved might be indicated by waiting for a chunk of granite to dissolve in a pail of water!

What gives this clay its unique working properties? It is not merely its chemical composition, for water and the oxides of aluminum and silicon could be combined in the exact ratio as they occur in clay, but this combination would possess none of clay's innate plasticity. It is, instead, a synthesis of a number of factors inherent within the mineral particle, such as its minute size and colloidal properties, its flat platelike shape which gives a sliding action of one particle upon another, its interlocking with other grains, and the molecular attraction of its surface charges for the charges of other particles. It is probable that the plastic idiom of clay is a concurrent result of such factors, the actual theory of which holds little creative interest for the potter.

One of the foregoing considerations of prime practical importance, however, is the grain or particle size, for it is perhaps this more than any other factor which determines the potentialities of clay as a plastic medium. There is wide divergence in the response of clay materials to forming techniques. Some clays are so sticky that they can be modelled and stretched and bent with little cracking or crumbling, others are so crumbly that they resemble pie crust dough, easy to compress into a mass but rather difficult to extend by stretching.

A safe generalization is that the smaller the clay particles, the greater the plasticity of the clay mass; the larger the particles, the less the plasticity. This disregards parallel considerations such as the amount of water combined with the clay. But whatever the relative size of this clay grain, it is infinitely small, measurable in microns rather than in inches. An appreciable idea of this grain size is offered by the Georgia Kaolin Company: ". . . [the particle] has the shape of a thin, hexagonal platelet, and is so tiny that 10 billion such particles, spread over a postage stamp, would form a layer thinner than a human hair."[3] The shape and size are indicated on the accompanying electron photomicrograph of kaolin particles, with a magnification of 16,400.

Figure 4. Courtesy of The Georgia Kaolin Company. Photograph: Electron Microscope Laboratory, Engineering Experiment Station, The Georgia Institute of Technology.

The earth forces which changed, and still are changing, hard rock into soft clay did not stop with kaolinization. They continue their slow, persistent labor. They move clay, deposit it, grind it, combine it with other materials, and levigate it. The two broad classes into which clays may be categorized are relative to such forces acting upon them since their transformation from feldspar. Those clays which remain at the site of their parent rock are termed primary or residual; those which have been moved are known as transported or secondary.

Primary clays vary in composition and properties, depending upon the degree to which decomposition of the rock has taken place. They are relatively pure, white-burning, and the chief impurities present are quartz and mica. Grain size is comparatively large, and thus such materials are not too plastic or workable. Iron impurities giving a yellowish fired color may be present if the parent feldspar contained an appreciable amount of that element. Deposits of such primary kaolins occur in the United States along the eastern seaboard, chiefly in North Carolina and South Carolina. Another material within this group is one which is halfway between feldspar and kaolin, a semi-kaolinized rock mined in England and known as Cornwall Stone. It has none of the plasticity of kaolin and has a higher melting point than feldspar. It is used in many body and glaze compositions.

Clays of the other broad group, the secondary or transported, vary in a number of ways from the primary. Rather than being located at their place of origin, such clays have been moved by natural means of wind, glacier, and most often, water. Consequently they are less pure, being admixed with other mineral and organic substances as they pursue their travels. The principal materials picked up are the iron-bearing compounds, evidence of the abundance of these elements and the prime reason why most secondary clays do not fire to a white color. Water-born and deposited clays are named sedimentary, and are usually much more plastic than their stay-at-home cousins because of a finer grain size. This is the result of the subtle grinding which occurs during their transportation, and also of levigation, the tendency of large particles to settle out of water suspension earlier than the finer divisions which are carried and deposited in quieter waters.

The classification of the secondary clay materials is rather complex, dependent upon elements of little interest in this discussion, but several main types merit description in view of their importance to the potter. There are a few sedimentary clays sufficiently pure to be white-burning and thus to be termed kaolins, such as those found in Georgia and Florida. Fossil remains often give evidence of the marine deposition of such clays and must be removed during the processing of the crude material, but these kaolins are tiny enough in grain size to make them of great value where workability, along with the whiteness of primary kaolins, is desirable. Another group of variable composition but of great importance for their working properties comprises the ball clays, sedimentary clays which have been deposited in boggy or swampy areas. Their unfired colors range from tan to brownish grey to almost black because of the inclusion of decayed organic materials, but when fired they are of a light buff or tan tonality after the carbonaceous materials have been burned away. They add workability and dry strength to pottery bodies but are much too plastic and sticky to be used alone, in which case excess drying shrinkage and cracking would also prove troublesome. Principal deposits in the United States occur in Tennessee and Kentucky.

Although none of the aforementioned clay materials can be used alone as a pottery body, those of another group can, namely the stoneware clays and the fireclays. They are sedimentary, varying in degree of plasticity and in fired color, but capable of being carried to a rather high temperature owing to low iron content. Free silica is usually present, and particularly in the stoneware clays, sufficient alkaline materials to provide a fluxing action are also present. When fired, pottery made from clays ranges in color from tan to brown to grey, depending upon the atmospheric quality within the kiln, and is often textured with a pleasing speckle afforded by iron-bearing "impurities." These clays have been used in many of the sturdy and homely wares which comprise one of the archetypes of pottery, the stonewares. Much of contemporary pottery, as well as that of Sung Dynasty China and nineteenth-century America, falls within this classification. It is characterized by a "high-fire" tonality, rich, subtle, often caressed by fire, and a great degree of hardness or density. It is of importance to note, however, that these same clays are often used to produce earthenwares of a softer structure and a creamy tone, the difference simply dependent upon the lower degree to which the earthenwares are fired and the consequent lower degree of fusion.

The secondary clays which are the most abundant and the most available are common red clays or shales, sedimentary materials of wide variation in composition. These clays vary in color as they occur in nature, from red to khaki to bluish-grey, depending upon the mineral combination of their iron content, but they invariably fire to a pink or orange color, and as the temperature goes higher, to the rich browns. The term "terra cotta" has often been used to describe this tonal range, and literally means "cooked earth." Indeed, the world of man has been widely colored by this cooked earth, for such common clays have been used for centuries in the manufacture of red roof tile, the common red building brick in its varied hues, paving bricks, architectural terra-cotta ornaments, and other applications where man has altered or created his environment. Also included is the mundane flowerpot (which is in danger of being superseded but will never be surpassed in functional quality by imitative plastic containers), and the porous drainage tile which must be laid under many agricultural fields to remove excess surface water.

Common red clay is quite plastic, often to the degree that non-plastic materials called fillers[4] must be added to reduce excess shrinkage, warping, and cracking. Such fillers include sand and powdered flint, and a coarse, prefired crushed clay known as grog. Common clays often contain silica impurities, and in some deposits, lime or sulphur. Such inclusions often limit their use to the low temperature range, for if carried too high, bloating and boiling occur as gases are trapped within the mass as it becomes liquid and glassy. On the other hand, the writer has fired red wares to the point where they are vitreous, with no bloating and little warping, and they ring like a bell when tapped.

An interesting use of such iron-bearing clays is as glazes. These clays usually contain enough "impurities" which act as fluxes to produce a glassy state when carried to their melting points. Applied as a coating to wares formed from higher firing clays, they melt to form a coating known as a slip glaze. Such blackish or brownish glazes have been used on many wares of nineteenth-century America, on countless jugs and bean pots, and on some pottery of the Orient, in Japan as well as in China. Deposits so used by American potters include some in Michigan, and that known as Albany Slip Clay which is found along the Hudson River in New York State.

This discussion of raw materials could be extended to a far greater length, for the resources of the potter are myriad. One of the delights of his art is the continued exploration of conventional, predictable materials and of new, unexplored ones for their potentialities. Many are not intended for ceramic applications, as are clays and feldspars and glaze coloring agents, but are produced for other uses and adopted by the potter. A glance at a potter's pantry might make one wonder as to the possible ceramic value of such materials as vinegar, wood ashes, sugar, baking soda, borax, or egg preserver.

All have their use to the potter, however, and often the success of his works, or the way in which they might differ from a current vogue or style, is dependent upon his curiosity about materials and methods as he evokes what lies inert, visible only within his imagination and often even a surprise to that.

FOOTNOTES

[1]A few organic materials are used, such as volatile oils in the application of overglaze decoration, the organic binders which give dry strength to otherwise friable or easily breakable unfired clay bodies, and the gums or other adhesive agents used to prevent the powdering before firing of glazes from surfaces to which they are applied. Such materials, however, are merely transitory aids, burned away in the kiln and not corporate in the fired wares. A few pigments used in

the decoration of some low-fired primitive pieces are also organic, being derived from plant materials, and after their application and subsequent firing, they remain as a carbonaceous crust not burned away at the low temperatures and in the restricted oxygen supply to which they are exposed during burning. The faded painting on some classic Greek wares suggests pigments not fired in place; some present-day ceramic artists are using synthetics such as Epoxy, neither fired nor inorganic, but perhaps more permanent than many low-fired agents; the "real Indian pots" too often purchased by gullible tourists in the American Southwest are often decorated with garish, water-based tempera paints. They are neither ceramic nor typical, with their thunderclouds and lightning flashes, of the rich pottery tradition of the area.

[2]The term "kaolin" is derived from *kao-ling,* a Chinese word for high ridge or hill where such clays were found in that country. Kaolinite is assigned to the specific mineral having the chemical composition Al_2O_3, $2SiO_2$, $2H_2O$, the most basic of all clay minerals. The materials known as koalins are clays which are high in kaolinite content, relatively free of impurities such as iron compounds, and thus white-firing. Synonymous with kaolin is "China clay," and the terms may be used interchangeably.

[3]*Georgia Kaolin Handbook.* The Georgia Kaolin Company, Dry Branch, Georgia.

[4]Archaeologists apply the name "temper" to such materials in their discussions and mention crushed shell, mica, sand, finely cut straw, or crushed potsherds. The term, however, is seldom used in the vocabulary of potters.

3

The Types

Figure 5. Earthenware Plate. Pennsylvania German (1762–1840). Courtesy of The Art Institute of Chicago.

As diverse as the raw materials and the techniques of the potter are the names which are assigned to specific types of his wares. Indeed, many such nominal terms are so vague and so wide in their use and misuse that they have become rather meaningless. The term "china," for example, is applied to tableware of many ambiguous types, with some prestige apparently innate in "fine china." Equally confused and confusing are the terms "porcelain," "semiporcelain," "vitreous," and "semivitreous." Many museum exhibitions of the 1960's have been listing a category, Pottery and Porcelain, but announcements of such shows fail to cite the qualifications of either type, and perhaps many of the ceramics in such exhibitions, as well as many illustrated within this book, might well be questioned as to their eligibility to even be classified "pottery" in the traditional connotation of the word.

Many variables are involved in the derivation or implication of a name assigned to a specific type of ware. The geographical location of the place of manufacture might be used, as Delft, a town in the Netherlands, or Bristol, England; it might be the name of a specific factory or manufacturer such as Wedgwood, Haviland, or Syracuse; the name might be that of the culture which produced the ware, as American Indian, Sung Dynasty Chinese, or pre-Dynastic Egyptian; or it might be an indication of a decorative technique, as majolica, enamel, underglaze, or slipware; and the body type is often the basis of classification, as porcelain, earthenware, or bone china.

Whatever the name or its derivation, certain fundamentals may be considered in any system of nomenclature which attempts to classify pottery types. These include the clay or body type, the degree to which it is fired in the kiln and the hardness which results from that firing; the type of glaze, if any, which is used; the decoration or absence of it; and the functional or decorative purpose. The term "Delft," for example, is applied to a ware made in the town of that name, of a relatively soft, buff-colored or off-white body, covered with an opaque white, tin-bearing glaze, and decorated over the glaze with pigment, usually cobalt blue. Such a description, however, considers no historical or artistic factors and remains rather coldly objective, ignoring the fascinating story of this ware and its attempt to imitate Chinese blue-and-white porcelains.

Basic in an objective description of a pottery type is a consideration of the body or clay from which it was shaped, including its color, its hardness or density, and its texture. Broadest of all categories and the most frequently found is that which has the almost too comprehensive title "earthenware." Typified by a rather soft and porous body which can absorb water and let it seep through, it ranges in color from off-white, tan, terra-cotta red to black. The usual firing range is at a low temperature, from the dull red heat of a bonfire, which burned many primitive wares, to about 2000 degrees Fahrenheit. Within this range, any glass-forming agents present in the clay are not melted to any appreciable degree, and the structure is consequently porous and non-glassy. Common red clays, however, often contain sufficient iron compounds to produce a rather dense product.

Earthenware may be glazed or unglazed, decorated or undecorated, functional or purely decorative or creative in intent. It is this type which comprises the major ceramic production of man, and museums abound in examples by many races of all times since the neolithic, including many sculptural religious or symbolic artifacts as well as pottery. These are the red, cream, brown, and black wares of primitive cultures, the utilitarian and sculptural ceramics of T'ang Dynasty China, the slipwares of the Pennsylvania Germans, to cite but a few. The present-day household is also quite a repository, with its porous red flowerpots, casual tableware, lamp bases, and unfortunately most of its bric-a-brac.

The realm of the decorative arts is far brighter because of the color palette available in earthenware glazes. The brilliant, luminous turquoise glazes of the Near Eastern wares, the fluid richness of T'ang lead glazed pots and sculpture, the splash of color on Spanish and Italian lustered majolica are all made possible by the coloring agents stable within this firing range.

Fired to a higher degree than earthenware and varying from semi-porosity to almost complete glassiness in body density are the wares of the stoneware category. Such pottery is often produced from clays identical to those of earthenware, with the fired difference due to the higher temperatures at which the fluxes occurring naturally in the clay or added as feldspars are coaxed into a sluggish melt. A stoneware body may be composed of a single clay or compounded from several, but often contains particles of iron, silicates, or coarse clay "impurities" which produce an ultimate stony or speckled texture or color variation. The color tonality is characterized by a subtleness, softer and richer than that of earthenware, the result of higher firing temperatures, and often, open flame upon body and glaze. Glazes are usually subdued in color intensity because of the limited range of coloring agents, but they are often richer because of the interaction at such heats between glaze and clay not occurring within the lower-temperature earthenware range. Indeed, a transparent and shiny stoneware glaze is far different from its counterpart on an earthenware pot and can have a rich and fat quality which keeps it from the frequent blatancy and garishness of the latter. Wares are frequently left partially or completely unglazed, the body itself often being warm and toasted in quality where caressed by the fire, and the glaze not being needed over a body vitreous in itself and thus impervious to water.

The work of many contemporary American potters has been within this stoneware range, particularly since the mid-1940 advent of high-temperature kilns of studio size. Many wares produced far earlier, however, are of this type, such as the salt-glazed jugs and crocks of nineteenth-century America, the dense pieces of Sung China, and some of the Wedgwood produced in England, to mention but a few.

At the end of the scale of hardness, ranging from soft earthenware through the usually dense stonewares, stands the aristocrat of the ceramic hierarchy, porcelain. One of the chief differences between the former two and the latter lies in the very nature of the raw materials of the bodies, for although the softer wares can often be made from one naturally occurring and impure clay, porcelain is always developed from

Figure 6. Stoneware Cookie Jar. Arthur E. Baggs (1938). Salt-glazed. One of the classics in American studio pottery. Permanent collection, The Everson Museum of Art.

a combined number of materials, as free from impurities as possible, and never from a single deposit of one raw material. Its basic constituents are the white-burning kaolins and the feldspars, romantically termed the "bones and flesh" of the ware. Pulverized flint is a usual third ingredient.

Of importance is the degree to which porcelain is fired, for some of the most dense wares are carried to dazzling white heats, with pyrometric Cone 15, about 2600 degrees Fahrenheit, as perhaps the top limit. This actually melts the body to a glassy state, through phenomena which not only fuse the feldspar but also develop different crystalline structures such as mullite from the silica and alumina of the clay. This is responsible for the characteristic translucency of porcelain, a capacity to transmit light, although not an image as does a transparent sheet of glass. Translucency is relative to the thickness of body wall, for a very thin section might transmit light, while a thicker one might be quite opaque. Such translucency is not a necessary attribute of Chinese porcelain, but a beautiful ring when a piece is tapped is reputed to be.

Other characteristics of porcelain are whiteness, extreme hardness to the degree that it cannot be nicked by a steel file, a conchoidal or shell-like fracture when broken (such as the flaked quality of an Indian arrowhead), and a simultaneous firing of wares with their glaze coatings, in contrast to pottery types on which glazes are fired at low heats on pieces which have been given an initial higher biscuit firing.

Porcelain bodies are generally rather difficult to work by the hand techniques, for their composition depends upon materials as pure as possible to achieve the aforementioned qualities in the final ware, and the purer kaolins are not the most plastic of clays; nor do feldspar and flint contribute workability. The addition of ball clay can remedy this, but as it in itself is not white when fired, such clay might add a creamy tone and is claimed to reduce fired translucency. Bentonite, an extremely sticky and plastic claylike material, is often added to make porcelain bodies more adaptable to hand techniques, but the majority of porcelains are formed by casting or other mechanical process to achieve an ultimate thinness of wall and thus a maximum of translucency.

The term "porcelain" is European in origin, although the ware itself had its beginnings in China. Porcelain as a descriptive title is derived from the Italian *porcellana,* a type of seashell, and was reputedly first applied to pottery by Marco Polo following his journeys in the East. The introduction of Oriental porcelain into Europe, where it be- came a possession to be treasured, led to many attempts to duplicate the wares. Such was the Netherlands tin-glazed Delft, white in glaze but not in body as the Oriental and thus rather superficially imitative, although its cobalt-blue decoration, also imitative, is not without a beauty of its own. Other European attempts include the Medici porce- lains, produced in Florence in the late sixteenth century, which in- corporated low-fusing glassy materials into a white clay body, thus making it possible to achieve translucency at a temperature far lower than that required to produce true porcelain. The mystery of porcelain remained such until the early eighteenth century, when a German alchemist, Johann Böttger, engaged by Frederick of Prussia to evoke gold from base materials to finance his military program, discovered the secret of the raw materials and the firing of white, translucent porce- lain. But this in itself is a long and fascinating story. . . .

Types such as the Medici and others which include glass as their bonding agent are often termed "soft" or "soft paste" porcelains; those of the Chinese type which have feldspar as the chief fluxing agent and thus require a greater heat than the soft types to achieve translucency are known as "hard" or "hard paste."

Much confusion seems to arise from the wide use of the term "porcelain" and its application to wares of many and divergent types. Some of the properties mentioned do not apply to all works which may legitimately be considered within this category. Certain wares of the Han Dynasty in China, often called protoporcelain, far from white in color and of a definite greyish tone and not translucent, are the har- bingers of this most elegant of wares. The term "semiporcelain" is widely used, particularly in the advertisement of tablewares as if it implies an

Figure 7. Scarab Vase, with stand and cover. Adelaide Alsop Robineau (1910). Porcelain, excised and perforated decoration. Permanent collection, The Everson Museum of Art.

"The Scarab Vase emerges as a work thoroughly representing its time. Its canopic form and scarab decoration bespeak the eclecticism of the period. The vestigial remains of *Art Nouveau* are certainly there, but much of what was to follow in the decorative arts is also surely represented in this amazing work."

William Hull, "Some Notes on Early Robineau Porcelains," *Bulletin,* Everson Museum of Art, 1960.

Figure 8. White Porcelain Bowl. China, Yuan Period (1280–1367). 1 15/16" h. Courtesy of The Art Institute of Chicago.

A group of porcelains, diverse in time, style, and method (Figs. 7, 8, 9, 10).

added value or worth, but objectively it simply means that its porosity and consequent absorption is greater than that of dense porcelain, although not to the degree of earthenware.

Many of the characteristics of porcelain are to be found in a body type designated "china," which possesses whiteness and translucency but differs primarily in the technicalities of its glaze. Whereas porcelain is glazed before its final firing, china is given an initial biscuit firing without a glaze to a temperature at which its body becomes hard and translucent. The glaze is applied to this fired ware and fused in place at a temperature lower than that of the initial fire. This process has the advantage of allowing the pieces to be supported during the higher biscuit firing by devices which would mar the pieces were they coated with glaze, and it permits them to be stacked, nested, or otherwise

Figure 9. Porcelain Footed Bowl. William Staffel. From "Ceramic Arts U.S.A. 1966." Photograph courtesy of International Minerals & Chemical Corporation.

According to the artist, "The piece was draped over a balloon in thin platelets of clay. Since the body is a mineral mixture made without plastic clay, plasticity is whatever I want it to be. Plasticity for working purposes is borrowed from organic plastics which are burned out in the firing, Cone 9. That's why translucency and whiteness are increased—no clay."

braced, or even fired cup lip kissing cup lip. This helps to prevent the warping incumbent in the unsupported firing of porcelain wares, and also reduces the per-piece cost of production, as less kiln shelf space is involved if pieces can be stacked.

While it is technically often difficult to note the difference between china and porcelain, the most obvious clue is usually the foot or base of the ware and whether or not it is covered by glaze. On true porcelain, it is impossible to cover the foot rim of a plate with glaze, as the piece must rest on its foot during the fire. Any glaze on the foot would fuse the piece to the kiln shelf, and any partial support away from the foot area would probably induce sagging or distortion during firing. On china, the foot rim may be coated with glaze and the piece supported by stilts or other refractory devices, possible because the ware does not reach the glassy softness during the lower glaze firing that it did during its original or biscuit firing. Consequently, china usually shows evidence of its firing supports, often insignificant little blemishes under the rim of pieces such as dinner plates.

Bone china is similar to the foregoing, containing in its body substance an amount of calcium phosphate or burned bone which acts as a flux to produce a fired ware of great translucency and of considerable strength even though quite thin in section. Unfortunately, bone china and china have suffered untold agonies in the hands of china painters and souvenir producers who seem to have little sympathy for the often beautiful austerity of form and material of their victims.

Figure 10. Medici Plate. Florence, Italy (ca. 1580). Soft paste porcelain. The Cleveland Museum of Art, John L. Severance Fund.

4

The Fire

Figure 11. Three identical sets of pyrometric cones, unfired, properly fired, and overfired. See page 31.

No discussion of the potter's art would be complete without consideration of his ultimate tool, fire. It is fire which imparts to his wares their final hardness, evokes the color and texture of glaze and body previously invisible to all but the potter's clairvoyant eye, and which in itself can impart its own fortuitous touch to pottery surfaces.

Physically and chemically, the primary purpose of the firing[1] of ceramics is to produce a hardness or glassiness which makes the product more useful and permanent, and in the case of pottery, more beautiful. Vessels of unfired clay, although appearing in their visual structure as if they were fired, would hold no liquids, for if filled with water, they would soon disintegrate into a muddy mass;[2] they would be so fragile or friable that even though filled with a dry material, they would stand little handling or jolting without breaking; even pieces such as sculpture whose only function is to be observed or contemplated would have a rather short life.

The hardness imparted to clay by firing is more than that of the sun-baked soil so resistant to the gardener's hoe in August, although adobe bricks of unfired clayey earth, often interlaced with straw, have long been used as a time- and element-defying building material in arid locations. The clay materials, before firing, can be combined with water to a workable consistency, then can be dried out and moistened again, and subsequently thus reworked almost indefinitely, losing plasticity only through the removal of fine-grained particles. Such procedures do not alter the basic chemical or mineral structure of clay. The water which affords the clay mass plasticity is combined in a mere physical mixture with the clay particles in varying amounts and produces the stages of workability discussed in the section on forming techniques. It is actually the only variant between liquid slip, plastic, leather-hard, and bone-dry clay.

But also within the clay substance is water which is chemically locked within the mineral crystal, and it is there in a constant ratio despite the physical wetness or dryness of the material. This combined water can be removed only by the elevated temperatures of red heat, and once removed can never be replaced. It is interesting to note that a mass of powdered clay heated to a low red heat and mixed with water after cooling will not possess the workability it otherwise would have had before firing, nor will it form a slip if combined with sufficient water to be fluid, but will settle out of suspension.[3] This is one of the theories which explains the plastic idiom of clay, that of its chemically combined water. Simple removal of this water with no alteration of other major factors, such as grain size, removes the workable property.

Much primitive pottery, fired to a relatively low degree in open bonfires or within crude kilns, has reached only this stage, and is merely physically and chemically dehydrated rather than fused to any substantial degree of hardness. It is, on the other hand, this degree of openness or porosity which imparts to such low-fired wares their capacity to cool water. The evaporation of a liquid is an endothermic (heat-absorbing) process, and the slow evaporation of water from the surface of porous wares through which it seeps is a natural cooler for the contents of the pots.

The degree to which pottery may be fired and the density resulting are primarily controlled by the glass-forming agents, the fluxes, present in the clay body. Such fluxes may be mineral "impurities" occurring naturally in the clay, such as compounds of iron, of lime, or of the alkalis sodium and potassium, or they may be introduced into the clay batch as it is prepared. These added materials include the feldspar which is so important in porcelains, the bone ash in bone china, and even glass in soft paste porcelains. The clay body is not the only consideration in the firing range, for when glazes are used over it, the relationship between the fusion point of the glaze and that of the body is also of importance. A high-temperature porcelain glaze, for example, cannot be used on a pot made of common red clay, for the glaze would achieve little fusion before the pot would have melted out beneath it.

The firing cycles of pottery bodies and glazes might be explained in steps of dehydration (water removal), oxidation of certain substances, arrested fusion after allowing the temperature to reach a degree corresponding to a desired action on fluxes in clay and glaze, followed by a period of cooling.[4] Such steps in the firing cycle are variable from clay to clay and from glaze to glaze, so to theoretically follow any one through the inferno would not be indicative of the course of others. The common red clay flowerpot, however, composed as it is of a clay which has an average composition comparable to that of the crust of the earth itself, would perhaps be the most typical.

It is mandatory that the wares be dry before firing, free as possible from all physically combined water. This can be accomplished by natural or gently forced drying outside of the kiln, or by a very slow initial heating after the pots are placed within it. If water within the clay substance is converted to steam more rapidly than it can escape, the piece is apt to be shattered, or splitting or cracking may result from uneven, rapid drying.[5] Small air pockets may fill with steam and produce similar unhappy results, and it is for this reason that careful wedging or de-airing of clay before it is formed is essential. As the temperature within the kiln begins to rise, the physical dehydration wanes as chemically combined water is driven off in the range of red heat. Also, as this stage of incandescence is approached, any compounds of sulphur, carbon, or iron begin to be oxidized or burned. Here the common red clay pot begins to assume the chemical composition which will eventually be responsible for its final color, for when put into the kiln, it may have been blue-grey, khaki green, or yellowish-brown in hue, depending upon the chemical combination of the iron in the raw clay, usually a hydroxide or carbonate if the clay was nonred, or an oxide form if red.[6] If insufficient oxygen is present, a blackish color due to FeO (black ferrous oxide) might result, as evident on some pieces burned in an open fire. Some blackness of such wares might also be due to carbon deposits.

As the temperature continues to rise, the fluxes begin their melting, a complex action of these agents resulting in the glassy bond which gives to ceramics their fired strength. It is within this range, about 1700 to 2000 degrees Fahrenheit, that the hypothetical red flowerpot will reach a stage of fusion which will make it quite strong when cooled, but not glassy to the degree that it will be impervious to the passage of air and water, so important to the life of its future occupants. Carried still higher, fluxes would develop glassy compounds, and the piece might become quite dense and impervious to water. The ring produced when some hard-burned red wares are struck can be a pleasant musical sound, often more resonant than the sound of porcelain, the avowed prima donna of the pottery stage.

With a further increase in heat intensity, the entire volume of the flowerpot would begin to boil and bloat as gases generated by materials reaching their vaporization points are trapped within the now glassy mass, and the texture would resemble that of a bubbling griddle cake. Ultimately the entire form would collapse as a fluid state is approached, with insufficient viscosity to support its mass, and the resulting blob would resemble even more the aforementioned pancake.

This melting capacity of the red clays from which the humble flowerpot was formed is not always deleterious, for when controlled it is the basis of the beautiful slip glazes discussed in the chapter on raw materials. As is true of so many of the potter's techniques, tools, and materials, it is within his hands and his imagination that their potentialities are evoked, and it is in his fire that they are finally realized.

The necessity for foresight by the potter is one vital way in which his art differs from that of artists in other media. Although his hands are more directly involved in his production than are those of the painter, the metalworker, or the sculptor, his work never reaches its ultimate form under his hand or within his sight. His clay as he works it may be grey, greenish, or red, but the same clay upon emergence from the kiln may have changed from grey to white, from green to red, or from red to black. His slips and glazes at the time of their application to the wares may seem colorless, dusty coatings, seldom with any potent color, yet after their processing within the kiln, they may appear glossy or velvety or dull in surface, deep and rich in color or of a soft and subtle tonality, speckled in texture or monotonously even, transparent or opaque, as the kiln invokes its magic upon them. This metamorphosis within the confines of the kiln requires a certain clairvoyance on the part of the potter, as he must look ahead to the finality he can only imagine or anticipate but cannot at the moment actually see beneath his hands as they work.

This is one of the most fascinating aspects of the potter's craft, whether he be a rank amateur or a skilled artisan, that the flame itself is final tool to leave a mark on the ware. The time between the turning off of the heat source, through the cooling stage to the degree of temperature at which the kiln may be safely "cracked" without producing that action on the part of the cooling wares within, is one of great anticipation to any potter, no matter what his degree of experience. Although the skills involved in the manipulation of this tool of fire are as important as any other of the potter, his pots hot out of the kiln are often a surprise and always an excitement. Few studio potteries are without a well-used pair of asbestos gloves, holey evidence of a potter's birth pangs, despite the warnings in most pottery texts that wares should be left in the kiln until they can be safely handled with the bare hands.

An exception is raku, a Japanese technique[7] involving the application of low-firing, usually lead-bearing, glazes to porous, low biscuit-fired pieces, and placing of the freshly glazed pieces directly into a preheated, red-hot kiln, preheating the wares only to dry the glaze coating. This slights the usual slow warming of wares within the kiln, as well as that of the usual cooling period, for pieces are withdrawn with tongs when their glazed surfaces appear fluid and melted, and are often immersed while still incandescent into water or into organic materials such as sawdust to achieve crackled or charred effects. Raku bodies must be composed to withstand the heat shock of such treatment, for most clay bodies would crack upon such rapid and uneven cooling.

There are many ways in which the action of the fire on the wares results in a quality of body or glaze which serves as a reminder that this fire, evanescent as it may seem, is too an important part of the final piece. This is seldom evident in mass-produced wares, in which any mark of the flame, producing any unevenness or flaw, would usually mean a reject or a "second" on the inspection line. An exception might be the quality of some flashed brick or sewer tile, often rich and varied in fired quality but too often returned to the earth from which they came. In the work of the potter-craftsman, such touches can add a warm quality and a feeling of finality approached in few other media. Pots fired in open flame are often caressed by black marks of the flame's tongue (Figs. 48, 76); glazes may be uneven in color or texture, more exciting because of their tonal variation than they would be if evenly fired; much stoneware by contemporary potters has a warm and toasted quality where their iron-bearing bodies have received a flash on unglazed areas or a speckled quality where the ashes of burning wood are wafted through the firing chamber and deposited on the receptive surfaces of incandescent pots.

Although the physical and chemical technicalities involved in fire and firing are beyond the objectives of this work, several suggest a cursory mention in view of their primacy in the esthetics of the pottery arts. One of the important, if not the most important, necessities in the production of pottery is the means of firing, be it a crude bonfire or a refined kiln, for any clay shaped into a pot still remains clay until fire transforms it. Kiln structures are of many types, and even those of the same general type can vary greatly in their physical forms, depending upon the type of ware fired, the number in which such wares are produced, the fuel consumed by the kiln, the degree of heat desired, and in other ways.

Perhaps the most simple means of firing involves no actual kiln structure whatsoever, this being the open or slightly restricted fire in which wares have been fired by most primitive potters. Such fires, of course, produce no great degree of hardness in wares. Kilns in themselves must be structured of materials with refractory properties, refractory being a descriptive term assigned to materials relative to their capacity to withstand elevated temperatures. It is a relative term in that such materials are refractory only in comparison with one another. Bricks formed from common red clay, for example, might be sufficiently refractory to be used in the construction of a kiln for low-fired earthenware, but the same brick would melt if stoneware or porcelain were fired in such a kiln, perhaps before the pots it contained even approached the degree of fusion desired.

As well as being refractory, kilns must have some capacity to contain or retain the heat generated within them. To meet this need, kiln structures include some insulating materials to prevent heat loss, thus holding the heat within and enabling it to build up to a desired degree. Such materials usually incorporate dead or trapped air space and are similar in their function to fluffy materials such as certain asbestos and spun glass products used to insulate buildings, and to the fibrous clothing worn to insulate the human body. They differ from these materials, however, in that they must be refractory, for a kiln insulated with fiberglas would have its insulation reduced to a molten mass, thus firing the kiln rather than its contents.

Many kilns in use at the present time are constructed of insulating firebrick, a light, porous, rather crumbly material produced by firing clay which has been combined before its firing with a combustible material such as sawdust, the sawdust burning out and leaving behind a porous structure. This material has greatly reduced the bulky size of kilns and is now used in practically all kilns, particularly those of the electric type used in school pottery shops and by potters who work in a rather limited volume or under conditions which do not permit an actual fire. The use of such materials is not mandatory, for their invention is certainly recent in the long story of pottery and kilns, but such refractories make firing a much more efficient and economical process. It is a quieting thought, however, to consider that many of the beautiful wares which highlight the history of the potter's art were produced well before the day of modern technology and its many ingenious developments which make possible such efficient and controlled manipulation of fire.

The fuels used in the firing of kilns are several, and the structure of any kiln depends primarily upon the type of fuel involved. Longest in use has been wood, but this has been largely replaced by more handy means such as gas and oil, and more recently, electricity.

Kilns fired by the oxidation or burning of the carbon, hydrocarbon and cellulose fuels require a firebox in which to burn such solid materials as coal and wood, or a combustion chamber for gas, as well as a stack or chimney to permit the escape of the products of combustion, carbon dioxide and water, and of other gaseous substances released during firing. The stack also provides a draft or draw of flame through the kiln, and its damper is an important means of controlling the atmosphere within the kiln itself.

Electric kilns, in contrast, require neither firebox nor stack, although some venting is necessary to permit the escape of water vapors. Such units are less complicated to install than their fuel-burning counterparts, and some are so automated that they require a minimum of attention while being fired, and even turn themselves off at preset levels of temperature. This is true of few other types, all of which demand almost constant baby-sitting. It might be noted, however, that the more refined and controlled the firing system, the less the mark of the fire on the pottery. Glazes and bodies fired in an electric kiln are often rather sterile in quality, whereas those from a flame-consuming kiln are often marked by that flame. Identical glazes on pots of an identical body, some fired in a gas or wood kiln and others fired in an electric kiln, are often so different in texture, color, and general tonality that their common denominator seems questionable. On the other hand, many beautiful pieces have been taken from electric kilns.

The kilns illustrated in Figures 12, 13, and 14 are of types widely used in the studios of artist-potters or in schools, and a photograph of a large industrial installation is included to indicate the scale of production of commercial pottery. The variation in structure is based upon many considerations, some of which have already been mentioned. There are up-draft kilns and down-draft, there are jack arch and sprung

Figure 12. Catenary arch downdraft kiln. The curve of this kiln is determined by a rope or chain suspended between two points. Inverted and used as the curve of the arch, such a curve carries the weight or thrust of the kiln arch to its base. Courtesy of The Rhode Island School of Design. Photograph: March 3 Studios.

Figure 13. Top-loading electric kiln. L & L Manufacturing Co.

Several kiln types (Figs. 12, 13, 14, 15).

Figure 14. Gas-fired muffle kiln, stacked for biscuit firing.

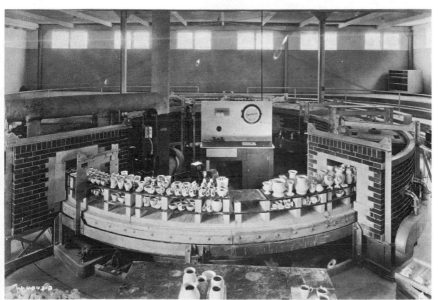

Figure 15. Thirty-foot diameter circular tunnel kiln used in commercial pottery production. The ware is placed on the "merry-go-round" cars which are constantly moving through the kiln. Such kilns may be as large as 100 feet in diameter. Courtesy of Ferro-Allied Engineering Division, Ferro Corporation, Cleveland, Ohio.

arch and catenary arch. In the latter the walls and top form a continuously curved surface with no division between wall and roof of the firing chamber. Some are beehive in shape, others rectangular; some are open-fired, exposing their wares to the flames, others protect them from the same element by muffle walls or by encasing them in refractory boxes called saggars. They range in size from a small bonfire or a small electric unit of perhaps one-half cubic foot capacity to giants resembling some fiery behemoth. Some are straight tunnels three hundred or more feet long, or merry-go-round tunnels one hundred feet in diameter, through which ware is constantly moved on cars or on sliding plates. Such kilns of the tunnel or continuous type are used only in volume production in which a constant supply of wares must be moved through a fiery zone of constant temperature, as are most commercially produced lines of dinnerware or sanitary ware (Fig. 15).

A number of questions seem perennial on the part of nonpotters asking for information concerning the potter's craft, and many such inquiries are directed at the mysteries of the fire. "How hot do you bake them?" "How long?" "Why?" "How do you know when they're finished?" "When can you take them out?" "How do you know how hot they get?"

Primarily, ceramists are not concerned with the mere degree of temperature measured in degrees, but rather in the degree of fusion which is reached by the wares being fired. It is this degree of fusion which determines when the firing has been accomplished, and the kiln is ready to be turned off—but not opened. To any such generality, however, there are exceptions, for in bonfired wares or in raku, little fusion results other than in the glaze of the latter, and raku pieces are withdrawn from the kiln while still incandescent.

An instrument called a pyrometer can be used to measure quite accurately the intensity of heat, but such an indication is one of temperature alone in units of degrees and tells little of the action of the fire upon the contents of the kiln whose temperature it measures. The stage of fusion of the wares and their glazes is indicated to the kiln fireman by the use of pyrometric cones, which tell not the specific temperature but rather the effect of time and temperature. They are solid elongated pyramids 2½ inches in length (or 1⅛ inches for the junior size used in the firing of very small kilns), composed of materials similar to those out of which the pots themselves are made, and thus they indicate the effect of the fire on a ceramic material rather than on a mechanical device. This advantage does not always entirely remove the necessity or value of a temperature-indicating pyrometer, for the two controls are often used simultaneously, with the pyrometer indicating the rate of temperature climb or drop. The indication of the finishing point of the firing schedule is usually reserved for the cones.

Cones are placed within the kiln visible from a peephole or spy hole through which potters seem to be eternally peering. As the cones approach fluidity and bend over, they ultimately indicate to the fireman when to turn the kiln off. Kilns, unless equipped with automatic shutoff devices as are some electric models previously mentioned, do not simply turn themselves off but require turning off by human means. Pottery within an overfired kiln which has gone too high can appear quite a glassy and bubbly mess when the kiln door is opened, and even the kiln itself can have its innards melted into a puddle.

The distribution of heat within the volume of the kiln can also be studied by the placing of groups of cones in various sites. Such are not visible from the peephole during firing, but when studied after the kiln has been opened, they indicate inequalities such as hot spots or areas of uneven oxidation. A mechanical pyrometer, from its fixed place in one spot of the kiln, can hardly indicate such variations, although there are complex installations of pyrometers which can afford such information.

Cones are available, manufactured commercially, over a wide range of melting points. They are assigned numbers which, as numerical values, have nothing to do with their melting points in relation to any degree system of temperature indication. It is by notation of this number that a potter knows the firing range of bodies and glazes. Glaze recipes are always accompanied by a cone number, relative to the fusion point of that specific cone rather than to a specific degree of temperature in degrees. For instance, a glaze to be used on a red clay body might be labelled Cone 04; another for a porcelain piece to be fired to a much higher stage might be marked Cone 10.[8]

As few as one cone may be used to gauge the firing of a kiln, but generally three are employed. They are arranged in sequence in a plaque, the plaque itself necessarily composed of a material more refractory than the cones themselves. The first cone has a fusion point below that of the desired cone and gives warning that the kiln is nearing its finishing point. The second cone, when it has bent over to the point that its tip is level with the base plaque, indicates the end of the firing, and the third cone shows overfiring if it too has bent over. Experience with any specific kiln will prove the only guide as to the time interval between the bending of cones in a series, for this interval varies with factors such as the type and size of the kiln, the rate at which fuel is introduced and consumed, and the degree to which the fuel is being oxidized.

Illustrated on Figure 11 are three cone plaques holding the same sequence of cones: the first as it would appear before firing; the second with the warning cone completely bent over and the desired cone with its tip touching the level of the base and thus indicating the time to turn the kiln off; and the third cone almost erect. The third set was intentionally overfired, far beyond the range of the cones, which are thus melted flat.

Cones are used by potters of the present day throughout most of the Western world but are not the only gauge of firing. The experience of the potter or kiln-man can hardly be overlooked. His trained eye can approximate the intensity of the fire or the fusion of a glaze visible through the kiln's peephole, for glazes appear almost liquid on the surface of an incandescent pot and can reflect the image of an iron rod inserted into the kiln to check the degree of fluidity. Draw trials may be placed within the kiln in such a position that they may be hooked out by a metal rod as the firing progresses, indicating the condition of the wares still within the inferno. This method is often used to check the deposit of glaze on salt-glazed pieces. It is also the principle of the Wedgwood pyrometer, invented by that genius of English pottery, Josiah Wedgwood, about 1782. Draw trials were removed from the kiln and measured against a calibrated scale, with the end of the firing indicated by a draw trial which had reached a desired degree of shrinkage and thus a desired degree of fusion. Such empirical controls long antedate pyrometric cones and the mechanical pyrometer, for cones, introduced in Germany by Hermann Seger in 1886, are late-comers on the pottery scene.

"How long does it take?" The duration of the firing period is determined by variables such as kiln type and size; by the degree to which it is desired to fire the pottery and by the condition of that pottery as to its water content when it is put into the kiln; and by the technicalities of the firing cycle itself such as the atmosphere within the chamber or the definite cooling rates often adjusted to produce mat-surfaced or crystalline glazes. A small kiln takes less time to fire to a given cone than would a larger one because more heat is required to raise the temperature of the larger mass. It simply takes more time to raise any one kiln to a higher degree than it does to a lower one, and wares stacked within a kiln while still in the damp or green stage for initial or biscuit firing must be heated more slowly to allow water vapor to escape, even when the pieces are apparently bone-dry; firing cycles involving reducing conditions, to be discussed later, are slower because of incomplete combustion of the fuel which may cause temperatures to fall rather than to rise.

"And when can you take them out?" A few ceramic works can be removed from the kiln with the aid of tongs while still red hot, such as the enamels on metal whose metal bases can stand the thermal shock of sudden cooling, and the aforementioned raku. Most pottery, however, requires a longer period of cooling, and many pottery texts suggest a cooling time equal to that of firing. Too rapid a decrease in temperature is apt to produce heat shock, often due to uneven rather than too rapid cooling, causing contractions which can crack a pot. Glaze textures, too, are subject to variations caused by cooling, for a rapidly cooled glaze may retain entrapped bubbles of gas which might have escaped by a slower cooling or "soaking," and some glazes may be shiny if cooled rapidly, mat or dull if cooled at a slower rate.

Two terms pertinent to the technicalities of firing and often used in the description of pottery are "oxidation" and "reduction." To the chemist, such phenomena are described as valence changes resulting from electron transfer, but to the potter whose interest is not quite as theoretical, they mean changes in color and quality, with wares fired under reducing conditions being among the richest, most subtle, and most beautiful of pottery effects. Involved is the oxidation or burning of fuel within the kiln and the degree to which it unites with the oxygen of the air as it burns. Heat sources, with the exception of electricity and possibly nuclear ones of the future, are combinations of carbon, hydrogen, and in some cases oxygen. These oxidize or burn to form carbon dioxide and water. When such combustion is complete, the kiln atmosphere is said to be oxidizing, and the various components of the wares being fired are provided with sufficient oxygen to burn to their highest oxides.

But when the supply of air and its component oxygen is restricted or the kiln choked with too much fuel, the oxygen is insufficient to completely burn the fuel to carbon dioxide and water, and products of this incomplete combustion contain carbon monoxide and carbon. Each of these, particularly at elevated temperatures, is rather greedy for oxygen and will avail itself of it from any source possible, especially from certain oxides which do not have as secure a grasp of their oxygen atoms as does carbon, thus producing a lower oxide of these materials, or even removing all of their oxygen. Such an atmosphere is termed reducing, and is characterized by a lazy, smoky yellow appearance rather than the clean blue of an oxidizing fire. Through the spy hole of the kiln, deposits of incandescent carbon can be seen—to the writer a beautiful sight—and deposits of soot on and around kilns bear evidence of such firing. Some potters claim that such heavy smoking is effective; others insist that it is a waste of fuel. It is usually necessary to finish off a reduction firing with a period of oxidation to insure that all carbon has been removed, or dirty black glazes may result. Conversely, strong oxidation at this time might reoxidize the reduced materials. Fire, too, is a versatile tool, subject to the whims and skills of those who wield it.

The ceramic materials most gullible to this alteration by oxygen-hungry gases are the metallic coloring agents used in glazes, the most important and useful being copper and iron in their various forms.[9] The latter also results in variations in body color, greyish when fired under reducing conditions, tan or buff under oxidizing.

In the normal oxidizing fire, copper in a glaze will be in its cupric form, CuO, and give its typical blues and greens, the variation being due to the chemical composition of the glazes. The deep blues known as turquoise, for instance, are colored by copper in a highly alkaline, low alumina glaze, and if tin oxide is included, have a pastel opacity. When fired under reducing conditions, however, the copper will be combined with less oxygen in its cuprous or red oxide, Cu_2O, and the result can be copper reds, among the richest of all pottery colors. It seems a matter of question as to the actual state of the copper in such glazes, some sources stating that the metal is in a cuprous state, others that it has been completely reduced to the metal which remains as a colloidal suspension of minute particles. But whatever the chemical principle involved, this is one of the most elusive of all glaze color effects, with the same glaze capable of varying widely from pot to pot and from one firing to another. It is found particularly on Chinese wares, such as those called pigeon blood and oxblood, and on the softly dappled peach blooms, in a wide variety of purples, reds, and pinks, and on all too few present-day works.

The other important metal whose oxides may be varied by adjustment of the fire is iron, the most versatile coloring agent on the potter's palette. In an oxidizing atmosphere, iron compounds burn to their ferric oxide, Fe_2O_3, although many such compounds are introduced into the glaze already in this form. Resultant colors range through the yellows to the browns, and in body compositions, tan and ivory to the red of terra cottas and to brownish-blacks. In a reducing flame, some of the oxygen is given up to the hungry kiln gases to result in the lower or ferrous oxide, FeO, producing glazes of a blue or green or olive hue, and body colors of grey or black. Often such tonalities penetrate the entire body wall thickness, with a delightful pink flash at the surface where the iron is reoxidized during cooling. On other black pieces, the body color is perhaps due to carbon remaining on the surface or trapped within the clay. A combination of these two oxides of iron is also possible, Fe_3O_4.

Glazes within this color range are termed "celadons" and vary from the palest and softest of blues and blue-greens to deep bottle greens. They often have the quality of jade, a quality to which many writers attribute the high esteem of celadons by the Chinese during Sung and later times. Celadons are typically found on the higher temperature wares of stoneware and porcelain and are often enriched by the tonality or texture of the underlying clay body, picking up the brownish speckle of stonewares or the pearly quality of white porcelain, particularly at edges or over engraved decoration where they pull away to a thinner layer during firing, leaving an accent of a lighter value (Fig. 80). Such glazes are found in great and beautiful variety on Chinese wares and have been used to good effect by many present-day potters.

The term "celadon" is of European derivation, ". . . believed to have been taken from the grey-green colour of the costume worn by the shepherd Céladon in a stage version of Honoré D'Urfé's early 17th century pastoral romance *L'Astree*."[10] Another legend would have it taken from the name of Saladin who made a famous present of the ware in 1171 to the Sultan of Damascus.[11]

To this writer, celadons are as much a quality as they are a color, for although their color can be imitated, often at low temperatures by agents such as copper, nickel, chrome, or prepared stains, such imitations always seem rather artificial and superficial, seldom holding the luminosity or subtleness of the genuine.

Several other metals are subject to variations in kiln atmosphere and can produce different colors dependent upon their oxide forms in the fired glaze. Nickel usually affords browns or greenish-browns in an oxidizing atmosphere, but in a reducing one it can result in blue. Titanium, when added as the mineral rutile, produces tan, but sometimes can result in blues when reduced. Vanadium, in combination with tin oxide, gives a rather painty yellow in an oxidized glaze, but without the tin and in a reducing atmosphere it can result in blue.

Another of the rich surface effects available through reduction is luster, a microscopically thin layer of metal over a glaze, giving an iridescent sheen such as that of oil floating on water.

Such reduction firings are generally limited to kilns in which a fuel is actually burned and its combination with the oxygen of the air controlled, but some contemporary potters manage it in an electric kiln, in which no fuel is actually "burned," by stuffing the glowing kiln with highly carbonaceous reducing materials such as moth balls, oily rags, or wood, and allowing the ensuing sooty smoke to do the oxygen stealing. This can produce lusters and rich copper reds on glaze surfaces, but seldom does such a method get to the degree of penetration that it

endows the clay body with the richly flashed effects of firing with gas
or wood.

Other artificial techniques involve reducing agents in slips and
glazes themselves, as in the beautiful locally-reduced copper reds
produced at The Ohio State University in the 1940s by Arthur Baggs
and Edgar Littlefield, who used silicon carbide as the reducing agent.

This discussion perhaps treats the area of kilns and their firing rather
superficially and summarily, but so many structural, physical, and chemical elements apply that to treat them thoroughly would be well beyond
the scope and objectives of this short work. But as with the work of
any artist in any medium, his tools can best be used when understood
as a creative means rather than as a technical achievement in themselves. Perfect control of firing can often result in pottery that is too
perfect, as is much commercially produced ware, fired under such rigid
control that it lacks that elusive yet important quality that is so exciting
and unique in the craft of pottery, the mark of the flame as well as the
mark of the potter's hand.

FOOTNOTES

[1]"Firing" and "to fire" are the generally accepted terms for the heat-treatment
of ceramic products, whether by actual flame or by the flameless incandescent heat
of electric resistance elements. The term "burn" is sometimes used, a "hard-burned"
brick being one which is fired to the degree that it achieves an especially dense
or vitreous structure; adobe, although not a ceramic brick, is merely "sun-baked."
The term "bake" is frowned upon by most potters, who feel it should be reserved
for creations more digestible than their pots!

[2]Such breaking down of dry clay when soaked in water is termed slaking, a
much-used procedure in the preparation of clays.

[3]Clays thus fired are termed calcined and are often included in glaze compositions which require the chemical constituents of clays but not their plastic
properties. Coarsely crushed calcined clay particles are known as grog, an ingredient
used in stoneware or ceramic sculpture bodies to give porosity, to lower shrinkage,
for texture, or to impart color flecks.

[4]This sequence has been arranged into specific temperature periods, but the
many tables listing such information are at such variance with each other that it
seems best not to add to the inconsistency by including such a table here.

[5]The writer once saw Professor Charles Harder, erstwhile mentor of several
generations of potters at the State University of New York College of Ceramics
at Alfred University, trim and slip-decorate and then glaze a leather-hard plate
which he had thrown a few hours before, put it in the kiln immediately, and
remove it after firing, intact and a beautiful pot. Needless to say, he carefully
supervised the firing of the kiln, and such procedures are hardly recommended
for the novice.

[6]Such iron compounds are in themselves specific minerals, usually limonite
or hematite, and when occurring relatively pure are the important ores from which
metallic iron is reduced in the blast furnace.

[7]To define raku as a technique or a specific type of pottery perhaps overlooks
more significant implications of the term. According to Paul Soldner, within this
writer's knowledge the leading American exponent of raku: "As I know American
raku, it cannot be described as a technique as we do not necessarily fire in a
preheated kiln. We do not always cool it in water and we do not always smoke

the pot! What remains is a philosophy or a state of mind that for me places emphasis on the discovery of things not planned." Mr. Soldner offers a definition given him by an elderly Japanese lady: "It is a state of happy anticipation."

[8]Cone 04 bends at 1922 degrees Fahrenheit when heated at the rate of a 108-degree rise per hour, Cone 10 at 2345 degrees when heated at the same rate. There is no mathematical relationship between the cone's number and its fusion point, nor is there a regular progression in degrees between the intervals in the fusion sequence. For example, Cone 05 bends 34 degrees before the cone next high on the scale, Cone 04, which in turn bends 65 degrees before the next, Cone 03. The complete range of cones and their fusion temperatures has been so widely published that such a chart is omitted here. Temperature equivalents courtesy of The Edward Orton Jr. Ceramic Foundation.

[9]Lead compounds, used as the principal flux in many low-temperature glazes, are easily reducible to metallic form. Because of their usually high lead content, low-temperature glazes of this type are seldom reduced intentionally, and when it happens accidentally, they may appear as a dirty metallic scum. Copper lusters, however, may be accomplished on such glazes if the reduction is not too intense.

[10]W. B. Honey, *The Ceramic Art of China* (London: Faber and Faber, 1945), p. 74.

[11]*Ibid.*, p. 74.

5

The Forming

Manifold are the techniques of manufacture devised by man, but despite the complexity and sophistication such techniques have achieved, they involve but a few basic operations dependent upon the inherent properties of the materials being worked. Such operations are the cutting of rigid or semirigid materials and the bending of those which are flexible; the pressing or casting within molds of some solid materials and of hot and cold liquids; the distension by pressure from within a mass or the stretching by stress from without; the modelling of plastic or malleable substances; and the extrusion through rollers or dies by which the cross section of a mass may be altered with no actual removal of any material of that mass. Often a final product will involve a number of such operations or a number of parts produced by disparate methods, requiring assembly of its component parts. Such assembly methods may also be resolved into a basic few: friction, as in the use of nails; interlocking, as in dovetail joints or in weaving; fusion, whether the materials be hot as molten glass or metals, or cold, as with clay; or the use of a binding agent, as in the brazing of brass, the gluing of wood, the soldering of silver, or the use of clay slip to unite pottery pieces.

The craft of the potter involves most of these fundamental procedures of forming and assembly, perhaps to a greater extent than does that of the artist in any other medium with the possible exception of the jeweler and the metalsmith, and especially of late, the sculptor. The potter cuts and carves his leather-hard clay and bends soft slabs of it to form pottery walls; he pours liquid slip into plaster molds, or presses plastic clay into them by hand or, commercially, by machine. He models his receptive clay in a way few other materials can be handled; his potter's wheel and the process of jiggering spin plastic clay into myriads of round shapes. The coils used as the structural unit in untold generations of hand-built wares are formed by the extrusion or stretching of a clay mass, and often lose their identity as coils are "fused" into a smooth pottery wall during construction. And the traditionally important tool of the potter, his revolving wheel, involves many of the above procedures, often in combination, including pressure and modelling and distension as a piece is shaped from soft clay, the cutting of the foot ring when the piece is leather-hard, and assembly as a pitcher receives its handle, a teapot its spout, or a lid its knob.

Of great importance in all pottery, and of prime importance in that of the artist-craftsman, seems to be the degree to which the forming process is an organic part of the final work. Certain methods, such as those which involve molds or other mechanical, impersonal means, tend to reduce birthmarks to a minimum. Others, primarily those used and favored by the craftsman, can leave the wares with lively marks of their geneses. Such marks often differentiate between the vitality of the spontaneously executed piece and the indifference of the mold-produced. Indeed, it is often the obvious attempt to delete all evidence of forming from the latter type which reveals a lack of sympathy of the worker for his clay. Conversely, the gentle finger and thumb indentations impressed into the soft clay of a freshly thrown pot as it is lifted from the wheel require no erasure, for they are a part of the pot's very essence.

Identical forms might be produced by slip casting and by throwing, which methods are discussed on pages 41-43 and 46-50. In the molded piece, the evidence of the process is minimal, with the parting lines, left at the places of mold division essential to the removal of the piece, scraped or whittled away but somehow always leaving an apologetic scar. In contrast, the same form thrown on the wheel will bear a different mark, a mark which need not be removed nor justified. This is the spiral left in the clay wall by fingers or sponge, sometimes vigorous and at other times quite gentle and caressing. A sponge or throwing rib (a flat piece of wood or other material used to form or to smooth a clay wall) can leave an almost polished surface, but smooth though they may be, such surfaces too can seem spontaneous and unaffected.

Such forming textures can be completely removed by scraping, sandpapering, and other tortuous means, to leave a sterile surface. Why such smoothness is not always achieved or desired is frequently asked. The potter's answer is often that he is interested in the quality of his material and in its response to his manipulation, in its inherent textures and those which it can assume in being formed, and often in the richness such qualities might afford when fired and perhaps covered by a sympathetic glaze. Indeed, the plastic fullness of the spout of a well-thrown pitcher and the liquid ease of its pulled handle, the sharp cutting marks of the tool which carved with great surety the excess clay from the base of a thrown bowl to form its foot ring—all such marks are a part of the potter's vocabulary, and the more such marks seem unassumed and spontaneous, the greater the vitality of the pottery.

Figure 16.

Figure 16 shows two geometrically similar forms, thrown on the potter's wheel using the same clay body. The form on the left was smoothed with a wooden rib, the other allowed to retain its pattern of finger marks incidental to the throwing technique. The same glaze covers each form. It is hoped that the two examples illustrate that effect does not depend upon objective similarities in clay, method, and glaze, nor upon geometric form, but rather upon the artist's control and use of such elements.

The factors discussed in a preceding chapter which determine the unique working properties of clay are also paramount in the use of this material as a creative means. A clay or clay body which is coarse, gritty, and basically nonplastic might readily lend itself to forming techniques and to forms which involve building up with small units or masses of clay rather than being stretched from a single mass. Some massive and sturdy pieces of ceramic sculpture, for example, are developed by using small dabs or smears of coarse clay. The same material, however, because of its lack of fine particles and thus of plasticity, might tear or sag or slump if thrown on the potter's wheel. Similarly, most kaolins, although burning to a sterile degree of whiteness desired in porcelains, are difficult to throw or model because of their large grain size and consequent lack of workability. When such kaolins are combined with the other nonplastic ingredients necessary in porcelain compositions, the resulting body demands forming techniques which require little plastic manipulation. This is to a certain extent responsible for the dearth of hand-modelled or thrown porcelains.

One important variable which can be adjusted by the craftsman is the amount of water which is mechanically mixed with his clay. As has been previously discussed, a fixed ratio of water is chemically locked within the clay crystal and is always there in the same ratio despite the amount of water added to give the clay mass a desired consistency for workability. In contrast to this definite ratio of chemically combined water, that of physically or mechanically combined water is quite variable. If it is present in an amount sufficient to give clay a fluid consistency, approximately 50:50 although this will vary considerably with clay types and particle sizes, the mixture is termed slip. If the clay:water ratio is in the range of 75:25, the mixture is usually quite plastic and workable, again depending upon variations in the clay involved. If the ratio is about 90:10, a stage quite descriptively termed leather-hard or cheese-hard, the mass is too stiff to be modelled or shaped without cracking, but it may be formed by the use of pressure molds or dies, and pottery wares in this condition may be readily trimmed and carved. Pressure molds are seldom used by the individual craftsman, but are widely used in the commercial production of flat tile, electrical porcelain, some dinnerware, and the common red clay flowerpot. Often such ram presses shape clay in a stage even drier than leather-hard, the clay containing so little water that it seems quite dry to the touch.

It is in the slip and plastic stages that clay is most often used by the potter in the production of his work. Slip is the agent used to attach one clay part to another, as a handle to a cup or a spout to a teapot, is among the most ancient means of colored decoration, and is cast into molds when large numbers of identical items are desired. Unfortunately, the latter technique of slip casting is too often employed by those who seem content to merely fill and refill molds, molds usually made by professionals and often of questionable esthetic merit, and to accept the impersonal outcome as their own "creative" work.

Although slip casting is not at the present time as frequently employed by craftsmen as are the plastic methods, the ceramic world is so highly populated by wares thus formed, some of which are high on the scale of craftsmanship and beauty, that a brief description of the method seems merited. The technique is based upon the capacity of porous materials to absorb water from clay slip, thus stiffening it. The principal mold material is plaster of Paris, although molds of soft-burned clay (biscuit) are another possibility. The molds vary in complexity from one-piece units for the casting of simple, open shapes to some which involve a number of interlocking but separable sections, the manifold structure necessary to facilitate the removal of cast pieces whose surfaces or forms contain undercuts. For instance, such a sectional mold used in the casting of a seemingly simple teapot might consist of numerous pieces to make possible the removal of the complete piece intact with its handle, raised foot, the lip on which its lid will rest, and its hollow pouring spout. It is also necessary that the mold be reusable and not expended, as is the waste mold of the sculptor.

Wares of two structural types are possible with this technique. The pieces which are called hollow ware have a wall of consistent thickness. This is produced by allowing the casting slip[1] to remain in the absorbent mold long enough for sufficient water to be absorbed from the slip to produce a wall of the desired thickness. The longer the slip remains in the mold, the thicker becomes the wall. The still liquid portion of the slip is then poured off, leaving behind that which has stiffened by the removal of its water. This layer of clay on the mold interior appears as a "lining," but it subsequently shrinks away from the mold as it drys, and releases itself.

Pieces which are solid cast are formed by allowing the slip to remain in the mold without draining, thus building a dense rather than a hollow structure, similar to the process employed in a metal foundry or in the molds used in casting toy lead soldiers or the bullets used by real ones. Often details such as cup handles are formed by this method and are subsequently attached to basic cup shapes formed by another.

In hollow or drain cast pieces, the ware is limited to a wall of consistent thickness, and consequently any variation on the outer surface of a form will be evident on the inner. A raised ornament, for instance, on the outside of a cast piece will be evident as a depression on the inner, and a flat plate with a foot ring on its base will have a ditch on its inner surface which follows in the footprint of the outer. Such a depression, needless to say, does little to uplift the quality of the form.

Structurally, a piece which incorporates details such as a handle will have a dimple (but hardly a beauty mark!) on its inner surface directly opposite the conjunction of handle and body, whereas a handle which is cast separately and subsequently attached will be without this inner depression. Such a mark is caused by the lack of an absorbent mold wall at this point. Similarly, a spout cast directly on a teapot can have no built-in strainer, but a teapot cast apart from its spout, with that rather necessary appendage formed separately in another mold, can have its straining holes punctured in before the spout is affixed. Such considerations hardly apply to hand-formed pieces, unless there is a slight depression on the inside of a cup or a pitcher marking the counterpressure applied to support the wall of the piece when its handle is pressed onto the outside surface. But in this case, the dimples are beauty marks.

Most of the hollow wares on the commercial and the so-called "gift ware" markets have been produced by this slip casting process, including teapots, sugar bowls and creamers, hosts of grotesque cookie jars and lamp bases, and unfortunately, most of the bric-a-brac.

If the potter who delights in the feel of his clay within his hand is apt to look with disdain upon the method and the product of the slip mold, it is perhaps because the final piece is always a substitution for an original developed in an alien material, usually plaster, which is transitory rather than permanent, with the original form being recorded in molds and then discarded only to be propagated in a substitute material. Many craftsmen are so beautifully skilled in the hand techniques that they can produce without molds any number of pieces which are practically identical, the only differences being those subtle inflections which give each piece its slight personal variation from the masses.

The plastic condition of clay, in which its water content is less than that of slip, is a variable one, but its basic characteristic is its capacity to be shaped or modelled and to retain that shape after the forming pressure has been removed. This capacity depends not only upon the physical properties of the clays which make one more workable than another, but also upon the personal preferences of potters and the techniques which they employ. Some work with clay in a condition like that of soft mud, barely able to stand by itself when shaped; others prefer it so stiff that it is almost leather-hard, requiring rigid force to control it. But despite the variation of clays in this stage, it is with the material in this plastic condition that most pottery is formed, whether by hand techniques or by mechanical means such as the potter's wheel.

For it is with plastic clay that pottery had its beginnings, and it seems a matter of conjecture as to the time in the long evolution of man that he discovered he could shape the pliant mud so abundant around him, and that such shapes could be permanently fixed by fire. But whenever in the gloom of prehistory the art and craft of pottery evolved (historians approximate the development within the Neolithic Period, 10,000 to 6000 B.C.), this mud has registered a most permanent and often beautiful record of human ingenuity and creativity. Clay was the raw material of many artifacts produced by neolithic peoples, and clay pots are often cited as evidence of the transition of nomadic hunters to a more stable agricultural stage which necessitated storage vessels for foodstuffs such as grain. Included in neolithic ceramics are works which are zoomorphic or animal in shape, figures reputed to have been of religious significance as fertility symbols, pottery formed by modelling masses of clay, by beating it with a paddle, or by shaping it over forms such as rocks or gourds, and of particular and significant importance, by building with coils.

There seem many and varied theories as to the origin of this coil-building technique of pottery construction. Some anthropologists regard it as a derivation of basket weaving, for such pots often resemble that craft in the interweaving of structural members. Textures on the outer surfaces of some wares suggest that woven baskets may have been used to support soft clay walls during construction, and baskets have been found which retain patches of clay inside, indicating perhaps their use as molds or the addition of a clay lining as a means of sealing the basket itself. But whether basketry actually preceded pottery poses questions which are more pedantic than esthetic, and of little interest here.

No matter what the derivation of the method, coil-built wares vary considerably in technique, form, fired surface quality, and in decorative treatment. Some are rich in textural surface where the constituent coils have been joined with tools or fingers, leaving an almost fabric-like pattern overall or in restricted areas (Fig. 76); others have been burnished or polished, perhaps with a pebble, to smooth and often glossy surfaces, frequently enriched by colored slip painting (Fig. 88). Some are of an almost unbelievable lightness, some Pueblo wares of the American Southwest having walls little over ⅛ inch in thickness. It is of interest to note that many forms executed by primitive pot makers using this coil technique are round in plan, perhaps indicative of basket prototypes. All forms, however, are not round or nonobjective, and may be quite complex in form and involve subject matter.

The methods of producing coils and of incorporating them into pottery walls are several. In present-day craft classes, coils are usually rolled on a flat surface from a plastic mass of clay, or cut in strips from flat slabs and used as cut or softened by rolling. The writer, however, has seen the Pueblo Indians of New Mexico form coils by holding a mass of clay between the hands in a prayerlike attitude, and by a gentle rolling of this mass between the palms, a thick coil descends. These fat units are used as a means of getting more clay onto the pot and not as an actual structural element, for after having been joined to a previously formed section, they are pulled and thinned into the wall by a squeezing action. The resulting surface is smooth rather than corrugated as in other coil methods, and is often made smoother with a tool, such as a piece of gourd, and given a final polish or burnish with a smooth pebble when almost dry. Similar incorporation of coils into pottery walls is achieved by paddling or pounding the soft clay into shape.

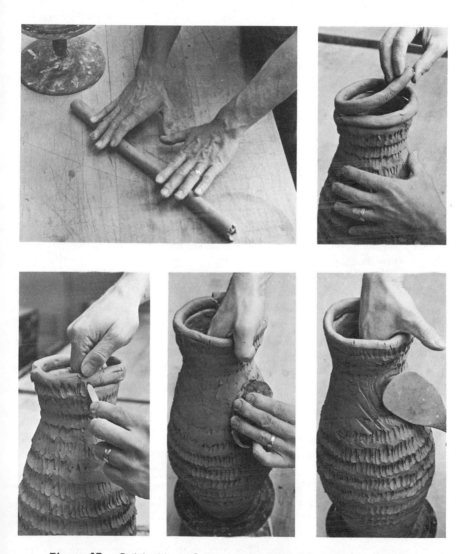

Figure 17. Coil building. Coils may be formed by rolling or cutting strips or bands of clay, and pots formed from one continuous spiralled coil or from a series of rings placed one above the other. Slip or water may be used to insure joining. The coils or the method of joining them may be left apparent, or the surface smoothed.

This ancient technique has been enjoying somewhat of a creative renaissance during the past several years, after hibernating in secondary school art programs, in college pottery courses, and in summer camps where it, along with beadwork and leathercraft, seems to bear some relationship to the American Indian. It is being used to shape pots almost gargantuan in size, far removed from their conventional, circle-bound prototypes. It is often incorporated with the throwing process on the potter's wheel as a means of adding more clay to a piece already in progress, extending height and volume beyond that which most potters can readily achieve from a single mass of clay. This method, however, is hardly new, nor is the mere gross size of the latest in coil-built giants, for the add-a-coil throwing technique has long been used by Japanese potters, and grain storage jars of twenty gallons or more capacity are to be found among Pueblo Indian artifacts.

Whatever methods may be used in the manipulation of clay in the plastic stage, none has been more widely used, produced more variations within its discipline, nor held more challenge and fascination for the potter than the technique of throwing on the potter's wheel. There are many stories concerning the origin of this almost magical wheel; many are perhaps legendary and romantic, but most seem plausible. That the wheel was a rather late development in the history of man, that before its adaptation as a potter's tool pottery was solely the craft of women, that it was not used in hoe-agricultural societies but was used by plow-agricultural—such broad statements perhaps lie within the disciplines of archaeology and anthropology rather than as conjecture here.

Joseph V. Noble summarizes the genesis of the technique: "The potter's wheel was invented near the end of the fourth millenium B.C. Its use was not immediately widespread, some areas adopting it far ahead of others. One of the first areas was Sumer, where it appeared about 3250 B.C. In Egypt it was used as early as the latter part of the IInd Dynasty, about 2750 B.C. In Troy, wheel-made pottery was found at the IIb level, about 2500 B.C."[2] The potter's wheel was unknown in the American hemisphere until the Spanish conquest—unknown was the wheel in any form.

It is doubtful that the concept of the revolving wheel as a clay-shaping device came in a blaze of genuis to any one man at any specific time, and more probable that it evolved from the necessity of rotating a coil-built piece to facilitate its forming. Present-day Pueblo Indians demonstrate the coil-building of a pot with the piece supported on a shallow, curved pottery sherd, the sherd nested into a slightly concave stone. The pot on its supporting sherd is spun with one hand while the other hand fashions the clay. The process approaches throwing, lacking the usual momentum of the potter's wheel, and the resulting pieces are amazingly round, symmetrical, and smooth.

"Throw," "throwing," and "thrown" are terms so relevant a part of any discussion of the potter's wheel that to refer to the tool without mention of its process is difficult. The words seem rooted in the Old or Middle English *throwen*, "to cause to turn or twist." Such derivation seems logical, for this is certainly the feeling of the spinning clay to the hands of the potter as it spins or throws itself out or up into circular forms. To the beginner on the wheel, however, the magical look of the skilled thrower at work soon loses it aura of sorcery!

Another theory of the derivation of the word is the throwing motion with which the potter slams a ball of clay onto the waiting wheel head, with force enough to adhere it to the wheel's surface to prevent it from tearing free when throwing pressure is applied. This seems rather farfetched, however, for a few loving pats can put a ball of clay in its place as easily as a powerful slap.

But whatever the lineage of the wheel or of the word "throw," the techniques involved are based upon a very few mechanical principles, subject to infinite variation. The wheel may be a simple, almost crude, structure, or one of exquisite refinement and balance. Basically, it is a horizontally revolving disc on which a ball of plastic clay is manipulated into a round form, hollow to some degree. The means of propulsion may be muscle or motor, with human-powered wheels usually involving a flywheel to achieve and maintain momentum. Such flywheels may be the actual wheel head, or a mass at another point of the axis of that wheel head. Some wheels are set in motion by the insertion of a stick into a hole on the outer top edge of the throwing head, with this stick used to spin the wheel, then withdrawn when the throwing begins using the achieved momentum, reinserted and respun when the wheel slows down and stops. Other momentum types are propelled by the foot of the potter acting upon the flywheel, thus allowing him to keep the wheel spinning as he works; although many do no kicking as the work is shaped but remove the hands from the work in progress to prevent body movement from throwing the pot askew. On other such wheels, a motor may be put in contact with the flywheel at the will of the potter, thus saving a good bit of treadmill labor (Fig. 18).

Treadle wheels are put in motion through a crankshaft device, with the potter's swinging foot propelling the mechanism, and at these the potter may stand or, on some types, be seated (Fig. 19). Wheels powered by electric motors can apply motion to the flywheel as noted above, or be a direct connection onto the shaft of a variable speed motor. At some of this type, the potter may sit and lean over his work; at others he can stand.

Figure 18. The Randall Wheel, Randall Pottery, Alfred, New York.

Figure 19. Klopfenstein Wheel, H. B. Klopfenstein & Sons, Crestline, Ohio.

The relative merits of such wheel types are a constant subject of discussion and often heated argument between potters, but a safe argument is that few thrown pots reveal the types on which they were thrown. Beautiful forms have been thrown on the crudest of wheels, and many a dumpy and dowdy form has been lifted from the most refined. It ultimately seems the choice of the potter to use the type which best suits his personal idiom, and often such choice is simply the one on which he first learned to throw and at which he feels at ease.

Although the mechanics of the wheel may vary in these many ways, essentially the throwing process is the same on any wheel. A mass of plastic clay is placed on the wheel head, forced—or eased—by an action termed centering onto the center of the wheel as it rotates, and then hollowed into shape. It is hoped that Figures 20 and 21 trace this process clearly. It is of importance to emphasize that throwing involves the plastic manipulation of clay, continually stretching and thinning a wall, distending it out or coaxing it in, to arrive at a pot's form. It is definitely not a process of removing excess clay by cutting the mass into a desired form as is the action on a wood or metal lathe.

Figure 20. Throwing a closed form. The ball of clay is centered on the wheel, pulled into a hollow cylinder, formed by pressure from inside and out, and cut from the wheel head.

Figure 21. Throwing an open bowl. The centered ball of clay is flared into a flat, hollow cylinder, and pulled out into the bowl shape. A wooden rib is used to ease the inside curve into a constant sweep. The plaster bat (disk) permits removal of the soft bowl from the wheel without distortion.

Figure 22. Trimming. The piece is allowed to dry to a leather-hard stage, is inverted on the wheel and centered, and clay trimmed away to form the base or foot ring.

Such a lathe or cutting technique is used, however, to execute the foot ring or rim at the bases of some pieces after they have been thrown, removed from the wheel, dried to a leather-hard degree, and centered in an inverted position on the wheel (Fig. 22). Many wares are completely devoid of such leather-hard trimming or turning, as the typical nineteenth-century American salt-glazed utilitarian jugs and crocks, many Japanese pieces, and much present-day American studio pottery. Often such pieces are removed from the wheel head after having been cut at the base with a twisted wire or thread, leaving a pleasant decorative shell-like pattern on the bottom (Fig. 23). Sometimes a soft rolling on a flat surface relieves the sharp edge of a cut-from-the-wheel pot and affords a gentle touch quite pleasing in relation to the pattern left by the cutting wire.

The capacity of leather-hard clay to receive additions of plastic clay or to be joined to other leather-hard forms extends the limits of

Figure 23. Bottom of a cup cut from wheel head with a twisted wire. Cup from The Leach Pottery, St. Ives, Cornwall, England.

Figure 24. A pouring spout is formed on a pitcher when the piece is freshly thrown and still plastic. The handle is "pulled" from a wad of plastic clay, and attached when the pitcher is leather-hard. Some potters pull the handles from a wad of clay after that wad had been affixed to the pot. See Figures 38, 49, 92.

Figure 25. A pouring spout for a teapot is thrown separately and attached when both components are leather-hard.

Figure 26. Lids may be thrown either inverted (left), or right side up (right). Some further work is usually required on the knob of the lid thrown inverted, although with skill some potters are able to accomplish this without much further ado!

Figure 27. Pots "thrown from the hump" are formed at the top portion of a mass of clay, removed by cutting, and the next pieces formed from the remaining clay.

A few throwing details.

---

shapes possible on the wheel. In traditional wares, plastic handles are attached with slip to more rigid pitchers or mugs, as are spouts to teapots. This principle is involved in many present-day ceramics which are far removed from functional purposes, making possible the sculptural treatment of wheel or otherwise produced volumes to be considered in the following chapter.

A mechanical adaptation of the throwing process is to a certain degree incorporated in the commercial pottery industry's technique of jiggering, which is used to mass-produce dinnerware forms such as cups, saucers, plates, bowls, and even oval platters. In this technique, the piece is shaped upside down, with a clay pancake draped over a revolving plaster mold. A template or profile, cut to the outside contour of the piece, is lowered to a radius position and trims or cuts the outside contour to shape. In the production of deeper items, such as

Figure 28. Jiggering.

cups and bowls, the rotating molds are hollow and give the pieces their outside contours, while the template shapes the inner. Such pieces are jiggered in an upright position, in contrast to the inverted position of a plate as is shown on the illustrations. The rate at which such automatons can spill forth their wares is appalling, especially on some which require only a supervisor to watch a series of conveyor belts, automatic water sprayers, lifters, and other Frankensteins do the work in a way that is less loving and certainly less costly than the human hand.

The molds can become almost as complex as those used in slip casting, with pieces such as concave cookie jars, casseroles, and bean pots being produced in sectional molds which allow the entrance, shaping action, and release of the template and the ultimate release of the ware. Such processes often involve the combination of techniques, as the application of a slip-cast or pressure-formed handle to a leather-hard cup, or the turning of that cup's flared foot after the cup is stiff enough to be removed from its one-piece mold. This makes possible the elegance of a high flared foot without the necessity of a complex forming mold. On other cups, such feet may be jiggered in separate molds and attached to the main form with slip.

This readiness of leather-hard clay forms to receive additions of plastic or leather-hard clay leads to an infinite variety of assembled, sculptural ceramics. Pieces may be thrown in separate sections and assembled when the constituents are leather-hard (Fig. 61), or a piece may be permitted to reach this stage with plastic clay then added and shaped in place (Fig. 47). This is frequently the method employed on bowls with a high thrown foot or base. A bottle might be formed by throwing the bulbous portion, allowing it to become rigid, and adding a section of clay which is then thrown into the tall neck form.

Quite different from these methods of handling plastic clay are those which involve the use of slabs or sheets of clay. These slabs may be formed by beating the soft clay on a flat surface, by rolling it out with a cylindrical tool such as a rolling pin, or by slicing it from a large block of clay. Such techniques differ from the throwing process in that the clay wall is preformed before the pot assumes any vestige of its ultimate volume, whereas the thrown or coil-built piece evolves as its constitutent clay is thinned or manipulated. Three-dimensional volumes may be developed from flat, two-dimensional slabs by bending them while yet plastic, or by allowing them to dry to a leather-hard condition, cutting them to shape, and assembling the semirigid units in a boxlike fashion (Fig. 29).

The bending techniques may involve a mold or other form, against which or into which the slab is shaped, or pieces so formed may depend entirely upon their own structures for support until dry, although a core of a removable or combustible material is often used with the latter. In the drape mold, the limp slab of clay is placed over a humplike form of a rigid material such as plaster or biscuit-fired clay, or a mound of moist sand. This slab may be cut to its ultimate outline before being shaped, or trimmed later (Fig. 31). Bowls and flat, platelike shapes have been executed by this technique, such as the Chinese Ting bowls formed over a hump which imparts not only volume but also a delicate pressed pattern to the inner surface of the bowl. Present-day artists

Figure 29. Construction of a rectilinear form using rather rigid clay slabs. See also Figures 52, 54, 58, 59.

Figure 30. Construction of a cylindrical form by bending a flexible slab of clay. See also Figures 35, 39.

Figure 31. Forming a clay slab into a flat plate by draping it over a plaster mold.

Slab construction.

---

also use this technique to develop hollow forms, with the component shell-like walls being preformed in sections and assembled when rigid enough to be handled. Similar techniques involve the placing of the slab into a mold rather than over it, or forming it within a suspended hammock of cloth.

The skill involved in the use of flexible slabs of clay to form standing pottery walls is evident in many contemporary American works, some of which assume an almost gargantuan scale. Often they strongly evidence the means of forming, showing an easy, wrapped quality quite remarkable in consideration of the flaccidity of the material at the time of forming, lacking any structural rigidity of its own (Fig. 39). Cores of combustible materials such as rolls of paper or wads of excelsior are often used to afford support to the soft clay structure. Such cores burn away during firing and thus require no removal other than a vent to allow them to escape as gases. This method is quite useful in the execution of ceramic sculpture.

Recent trends in ceramic art have indicated a marked and ever-growing freedom in the use of plastic clay techniques, particularly in the ways in which various techniques may be combined. Thrown pieces may involve coils, either as a forming method or as a means of getting more clay onto the mass of the piece to be thrown into its form. Coil or thrown pots may be augmented by slabs, and many slab constructions are lifted high on thrown feet. Such free and sculptural treatments are making possible works of a size and weight which would be difficult for the average potter to achieve were he to attempt them with a single mass of clay, and smoothly running wheels with powerful motors and little torque are taking a great load from many a potter's back.

Quite removed from these freely-handled ceramics are those produced commercially from a clay stiffer than that of the plastic stage by devices such as the extrusion machine and the ram press. They are beyond the intended scope of this work, but bear mention in view of their abundance in the contemporary human environment. Bricks and hollow clay tile ooze forth by the mile from extrusion machines which resemble giant meat grinders, making possible infinite walls of clay brick, hopelessly monotonous except for variations in color caused by inconsistencies in clay or in firing. A few architectural applications of hand-evolved tiles and other surfaces, fortunately, afford a note of saving grace where architects and building committees concede to a touch of the lyric. Presses stamp out in monotonous legions the sterile tile so in vogue at the present time on the walls of bathrooms, kitchens, and restaurants. Some are lovely and rich in color and texture, but many are as hopelessly uniform as architects' and interior designers' specifications demand, somehow lacking the versatility of the potter's palette and ideas.

FOOTNOTES

[1]In order to achieve a maximum degree of fluidity in a casting slip with a minimum amount of water, agents termed deflocculants or electrolytes are added to the clay-water mixture. For example, a combination of 60 per cent clay and other solid materials and 40 per cent water would probably be a thick mass and not to any degree fluid, but with the addition of a deflocculant in a seemingly small amount, often less than ½ of 1 per cent, the same combination would be quite fluid and pourable. Such a minimum amount of water reduces casting time and drying shrinkage and extends mold life. Commonly used deflocculants include the sodium silicate solution called water glass or egg preserver, and sodium carbonate or soda ash.

[2]Joseph V. Noble, "The Forming of Attic Vases," *Archaeology*, June, 1966, p. 174.

6

The Forms

Within a shapeless mass of clay lies inert the potential of an infinite variety of forms, but clay remains shapeless and rather useless until man evokes these forms and fire imparts hardness. To consider pottery form as an entity within itself would be rather meaningless, for the subject involves more than mere description of profiles or of physical mass or bulk but rather encompasses a synthesis of materials, of tools and processes, and of ideas. Pottery, as does any creative art, begins with ideas or concepts, whether functional, decorative, or purely expressive, and these are made tangible by the potter within the idiom of his means. A form might begin with a concrete idea into which raw materials are objectively coerced, with a nebulous idea which changes and grows as the form evolves, or with no idea other than that of improvisation. And how many pottery ideas have their origin during the improvisation to which clay so readily lends itself!

The physical forms which may be realized in clay vary from those which are singularly two-dimensional to those which are definitely volumetric and sculptural. The generic term "pottery" is usually considered to include all creative ceramics, whether the forms are flat as are tiles or volumetric as pots, and often ceramic sculpture in which subject matter, actual or nonobjective, is the dominant idea. Perhaps more logical would be the restriction of the term "pottery" to those forms which are three-dimensional and volume-enclosing, and to consider flat decorative surfaces and sculpture as separate entities. This is not intended to limit or discount the significance of the two-dimensional application of ceramic techniques, however, for the history of the decorative arts is certainly richer because of glazed wall tiles, mural decorations, and floor pavements, and these are similar in method and in result to those employed by potters on their wares. Nor are the forms encompassed by ceramic sculpture to be overlooked, for within this category lies a wealth of plastic expression, exemplified by nonutilitarian primitive artifacts, by Chinese T'ang tomb figures, by the della Robbia glazed terra-cotta sculpture of the Italian Renaissance, or by countless others including many of the present day. Often the dividing line between pottery and sculpture is ambiguous indeed, if it need be drawn. Pottery has often been described as sculpture reduced to its simplest form elements, and conversely, many works which might well be called sculpture, in consideration of their complexity or their involvement of subject matter, are well within the definition of pottery if function is a prime attribute of the latter. But questions posed by such definitions and differences are apt to be pedantic and of little actual significance.

A few generalizations concerning pottery form are possible, although they are so broad that they might well be applied to any three-dimensional art form as well as to pottery: All forms are based upon simple geometric volumes or may be resolved into such volumes; they may consist of one geometric mass or of a combination of such masses; they may be primarily straight or curved in the planes which define or encompass them. So obvious that it seldom bears mention, yet of prime importance, is the disposition of the major axis, whether it is curved or straight, horizontal or vertical in its main direction or movement, or singular or manifold. Equally obvious is the complexity of structure, whether it is comprised of a single mass or volume, or is an assembly of several. The first objective reaction to a form, other than that of its size, usually involves such elements as those mentioned, for a bowl might be first described as flat, a vase as tall, a jug as straight or curved, a nongeometric piece as angular or curving in its basic rhythm, or a work as sculptural because of the complexity or the arrangement of its constituent masses rather than because of any actual "sculptural" subject matter.

Such factors are not only basic in an objective or geometrical consideration of form, but are also traits in a pot's style or personality. They manifest the joviality of a plump jug, the severity or vigor of a stark and angular work, the gentleness of the sweep of the interior volume of a richly shaped bowl, or the austerity and aloofness of a proud vase. As with humans, such characteristics are not always flattering, for pots in their forms too can appear tired and dumpy, can sag or seem bloated, simply resigned to the hands of the inept or overly eager potter who doesn't give his clay a chance to speak for itself.

For the poise between the ideas which the potter attempts to manifest through his clay and the capacity of that clay to make tangible the ideas is, at least to this writer, the very crux of pottery form, and even of pottery itself. To avoid an academic attempt at an objective classification of forms and its consequent oversights, it seems advisable to pose but a few basic and traditional shapes and to consider the manipulation of these in particular as indicative of the potentialities of pottery form in general. These shapes are the cylinder and the sphere, thrown on the wheel or formed from coils or slabs; the rectilinear volume whose planes are relatively flat and defined by straight edges; the nongeometric or "organic" form which, however, can usually be resolved into a specific geometric entity; and the complex form produced by the assembly of similar or disparate volumes. Included within such shape-families are those which are nonobjective and those which incorporate some definite subject matter, whether through color or value pattern, subtle surface modulation, or full plastic realization.

Whatever the gross shape or geometric identity of a piece of pottery, its ultimate essence is hardly dependent upon that shape alone, but rather upon the treatment of the plastic elements which comprise the whole. Several such relationships might be stated in mathematical terms, such as the ratio of diameter to height or that of base to top rim, or the locus of the major accent of a curved wall. But within such relationships, the genus pot is open to many creative mutations, for differences in quality and that vague attribute termed style are more dependent upon the craftsman's sympathy for his material and his use of it than upon basic shapes and their measure. For a spherical jar can be taut and consummate or relaxed and humanly askew and yet remain a sphere; a bowl can flaunt a sharp and exact rim which strikes a note of controlled statement and geometric perfection, or wallow within a soft and undulating roll of juicy clay, each of which evokes a different bowl from the same form.

The illustrations on the following pages were selected in the hope that they might clearly pose the variables of personal style and craftsmanship, anonymous though the potter might remain, against the foil of an otherwise static geometric classification. Many other choices, of course, might have been made from the rich history of pottery, but a glance into the past and a survey of the present might reveal that many "new" forms are hardly new as forms, but new only as the artist embodies within them his personal idiom and ideas.

Cylindrical Forms

"All wheel-thrown pots are based on the cylinder!" This rather limiting and dogmatic statement, directed perhaps more often than any other toward the aspiring potter during his first and usually frustrating attempts on the potter's wheel, might simply be altered to, "Many pots are, in essence, cylindrical in form," to encompass a vast array of wares. The works illustrated on these pages, Figures 32 to 42, were selected to demonstrate variations within the discipline of the simple cylinder. Some are straight-sided or involve subtle or flowing modulations in such sides, others taper to become slightly conical in quality; others inhale a bit and approach the shape often classed as a "beaker," or expand at the waist to become more plump and jovial. Several have apertures at their greatest diameters, others involve transition across a shoulder to culminate in a small opening. In the latter, the sharpness or softness of the shoulder line and the flatness or plumpness of the shoulder plane itself are of prime importance in the sculptural essence of the total forms.

The examples, it is hoped, manifest some of the possible variations of this basic volume through the manipulation of profiles, of lips and rims, of bases and feet, and of the lids and handles which afford utilitarian as well as decorative values.

See also Figures 35-44.

Figure 32. Covered Stoneware Jar. Angelo Garzio. Photograph courtesy of the artist.

Figure 33. Pyxis (covered box for ointments or jewelry). The Painter of London. Greece, Attica (ca. 460 B.C.). 4¾" h. The Toledo Museum of Art, gift of Edward Drummond Libbey.

Figure 34. Tripod Jar. China, Han Dynasty (206 B.C.–A.D. 220). 7⅜" h. Courtesy of The Art Institute of Chicago.

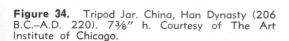

61

Figure 35. Slab Construction. Howard Kottler. Stoneware, 12" h. Photograph courtesy of the artist.

Figure 36. Vase. Korea, Yi Dynasty (1392–1910). White porcelain, clear glaze, cobalt decoration over the glaze. The John R. Fox Collection of Korean Ceramics, Syracuse University. Photograph courtesy of Syracuse University.

Figure 37. Salt-glazed Planter. Kenneth Ferguson. From "Ceramic Arts U.S.A. 1966." Photograph courtesy of International Minerals & Chemical Corporation.

Figure 38. Stoneware Cookie Jar. Robert Turner. From "Ceramic Arts U.S.A. 1966." Photograph courtesy of International Minerals & Chemical Corporation.

Cylindrical Forms.

Figure 39. Pot. Howard Kottler. Slab constructed stoneware, 28″ h. Photograph courtesy of the artist.

Figure 40. Stoneware Pot. Paul Soldner. Photograph courtesy of the artist.

Figure 41. Albarello (drug jar). Valencia, Spain, Paterna (fourteenth century). Majolica, 8¾″ h. The Cleveland Museum of Art, in memory of Mr. and Mrs. Henry Humphries, gift of their daughter, Helen.

Figure 42. Two cups, alike in size and function, slightly different in basic cylindrical shape, and far different in material and quality. Left, from Leach Pottery, St. Ives, Cornwall, England; right, commercially produced.

Figure 43. Stoneware Bottle. Peter Voulkos. White glaze, decoration in iron and cobalt, 12″ h. Collection of the author.

Wheel-thrown cylindrical forms are not ultimately limited to the vertical axis innate in the forming process. On the illustrated pieces, the main axis of each form has been shifted to a horizontal direction, openings have been cut, and details such as necks and bases added.

Figure 44. Bowl with Cross, Hagi ware. Japan, Monoyama Period (sixteenth century), from Yamaguchi Prefecture. Glazed stoneware, 9 9/32″ h., 12 3/16″ d. The Cleveland Museum of Art, John L. Severance Fund.

Spherical or Globular Forms

One of the most universal and versatile of all pottery forms is that of the sphere, whether by itself or in combination with other elements. Geometrically, it is the solid which encloses the greatest possible volume per unit of surface area, and it is this feeling of enclosure which is a trait of most spherical wares. Many receptive bowls are sections of this form, and other pieces which are partial sections often convey the concept of the total mass even though their planes or apertures physically subtract from such totality, for the human eye elides openings, one or many, and envisions surfaces carrying across them. Covered bowls and jars are often quite plump and globular, completely enclosed when their lids are in place, and many bulbous bottles almost entirely encompass themselves. Such rich forms are seldom geometrically perfect, but vary or may be altered in many plastic ways, as if by forces which seem to press them into flattened planes or areas, down into squat, pumpkin-like shapes or out into those long and ovoid. It might be noted that as the curved, spherical surface is altered by flattening or distending, the major diameter is also shifted, and as other elements such as lips and rims, necks and bases are added, the possibilities of the shape as a springboard for ideas become almost infinite.

See also Figures 47-51.

Figure 45. Pot. Paul Soldner. Unglazed, cast lead foot, low fired, 12" h. Photograph courtesy of the artist.

Figure 46. Stoneware Bottle. Nan and James McKinnell. Hand-built using coils and slabs. From "Ceramic Arts U.S.A. 1966." Photograph courtesy of International Minerals & Chemical Corporation.

Figure 47. Food Jar. Korea, Yi Dynasty (1392–1910). 10¼" h., 11¾" d. The John R. Fox Collection of Korean Ceramics, Syracuse University. Photograph courtesy of Syracuse University.

Above: "Simple globular shape achieved either by turning the two halves and joining in the shoulder area or by throwing the lower portion and coiling the upper part while still on the wheel. Opposite shoulders bear swirling floral motifs in underglaze iron. Clear glaze." Charles Ryder Dibble, Syracuse University.

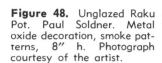

Figure 48. Unglazed Raku Pot. Paul Soldner. Metal oxide decoration, smoke patterns, 8" h. Photograph courtesy of the artist.

Figure 49. Stoneware Pitchers. Angelo Garzio. Simple globular forms, pulled into perky necks. Salt-glazed. Note quality of the pulled handles! Photograph courtesy of the artist.

Figure 50. Stoneware Bowl. Norman Schulman. A partial spherical form, dominated by a wide and flaring rim. Glazed on inner surface only, outer surface unglazed with impressed decoration accented by white slip, 13" d. Collection of the author.

Figure 51. Covered Porcelain Jar. Bernard Leach. Decoration in cobalt and iron, 3" h. Collection of the author.

Faceted Forms

Forms which are defined by facets or relatively flat planes vary from those which are quite soft and gentle in quality to some which are decidedly crisp and geometric. Precut slabs of clay may be used as the structural units (Figure 29); the sides of wheel-thrown pieces may be paddled or pressed into flat surfaces while yet flexible, or shaved or planed into facets when leather-hard.

Figure 52. Stoneware Slab Vessel. William Wyman. 26" h. From "Ceramic Arts U.S.A. 1966." Photograph courtesy of International Minerals & Chemical Corporation.

According to the artist, ". . . it has various overlappings of slip and glazes with scratching through to the body, and also wax resist. Finally, some oil color was rubbed into certain areas and scratches."

Figure 53. Slab Construction. Howard Kottler. Stoneware, 16" h. Photograph courtesy of the artist.

Figure 54. Stoneware Bowl. Contemporary Japanese, anonymous. Slab-built, 5½" square. Collection of the author.

Figure 55. Pottery Pillow. China, Sung Dynasty (A.D. 960–1278). Buff grey stoneware, T'zu Chou type, 7" h. Courtesy of The Art Institute of Chicago.

Figure 56. Small Faceted Vase. Korea, Yi Dynasty (1392–1910). White porcelain, 8-sided, cobalt blue decoration, 3⅛" h. The John R. Fox Collection of Korean Ceramics, Syracuse University. Photograph courtesy of Syracuse University.

Figure 57. Squared Jar. The author. Grey body, yellow mat glaze, 10" h. The piece was paddled into a square form immediately after throwing, and clay applied to the top and thrown into a circular rim when the bottom portion was leather-hard.

Figure 58. High-footed Bowl. Henry Lin. Sides and bottom slab-built, wheel-thrown foot. From "Ceramics U.S.A. 1966." Photograph courtesy of International Minerals & Chemical Corporation.

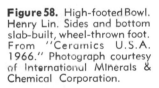

Figure 59. Sarcophagus—Ken Ferguson as Captain Mandrakus. Fred Bauer. One-half-inch slab construction with hinges and latch, brass pins, elm ash glaze. From "Ceramic Arts U.S.A. 1966." Photograph courtesy of International Minerals & Chemical Corporation.

Multiple Forms

Few pots consist of but one sheer form, but usually of one major or dominant volume to which other structural or decorative elements such as bases and rims are subordinate. More complex pieces may incorporate several major volumes, and their component forms may be of the same shape-quality or quite different. The archetypical vase or bottle, for example, may consist of cylindrical and spherical forms rising one above the other about a common vertical axis.

It is the axes of the component elements which provide the structural relationship of most complex pieces. Such axes may form a common line on which all elements are centered (Figures 60, 61, 62, 66b), or may cross at right or other angles (Figures 43, 66c). Forms may be joined with their center axes parallel but not common (Figures 63, 64); or with them slightly askew to result in a relationship of forms that is not so geometrically obvious, often reminiscent of the lush growth of mushrooms or other fungi.

And indeed this organic quality is often noted in the titles assigned to pieces, as in the accompanying gourd and tamarind bottles, but whether the pots were inspired by the natural forms, or the titles suggested by the final pots, is a matter of fascinating conjecture.

Figure 60. Gourd Vase. China, Ch'ing Dynasty (1644–1911). White porcelain, 20¼" h. Courtesy of The Art Institute of Chicago.

Figure 61. Tamarind Pot. Toshiko Takaezu. Stoneware. Photograph courtesy of the artist. The piece is named after a Hawaiian vine with a beanlike pod, and according to the artist,

"I threw three forms and at the leather-hard stage, I put them together—."

Figure 62. Urn and 12 Mugs. Don Reitz. Stoneware. The cylindrical mugs were thrown from the hump, and the flared feet added later. From "Ceramic Art U.S.A. 1966." Photograph courtesy of The International Minerals & Chemical Corporation.

Figure 63. Stoneware Planter. The author. Three inverted pyramid forms, 9" h.

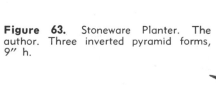

Figure 64. Meandering Multipot. The author. Five thrown stoneware forms joined in a line, added clay spines, 13" l.

Figure 65. Nine-pot construction, stoneware, Don Dunifon. From "Ceramic Arts U.S.A. 1966," courtesy of The International Minerals & Chemical Corporation.

a   b   c

Figure 66. a. Stoneware Bottle. John E. Ground. b. Stoneware and Porcelain Floor Vase. Vaea Marx. c. Earthenware Vase. Kenneth A. Hendry. From "24th Ceramic Exhibition." Photograph courtesy of Everson Museum of Art.

Figurative Forms

Not all pottery forms are purely geometric or nonobjective but may involve, to various degrees, specific subject matter. It is of importance to note that the forms illustrated here do not simply provide backgrounds against which subjects are placed in an illustrative way, but rather indicate synthesis of subject with form, ranging from subject indicated by subtle sculptural modulation or by nonsculptural color patterns (Figure 67) to forms which are completely plastic or three-dimensional in concept (Figures 70-74).

Figure 67. Pottery Beaker. Peru, Nazca. 8 3/16″ h. Courtesy of The Art Institute of Chicago.

Figure 68. Tankard in the Form of an Owl. Germany (1569). Earthenware and silver gilt, 7¼″ h. Courtesy of The Art Institute of Chicago.

Figure 69. Whieldon Teapot in Form of a Cauliflower, England (1740–80). Green and cream glaze. Courtesy of The Art Institute of Chicago.

Figure 70. Pottery Vessel in the Form of a Deer. Iran (Amlash) (ninth-eighth century B.C.). Painted terra cotta, 6¾″ h. The Toledo Museum of Art, gift of Edward Drummond Libbey.

Figure 72. Pottery Well. China, Han
Dynasty (206 B.C.–A.D. 220). 14¾"
h. Courtesy of The Art Institute of
Chicago.

Figure 73. Tureen in the
Form of a Turtle. France,
Strasbourg (1750–60). Faience. The Cleveland Museum
of Art, The Norweb Collection.

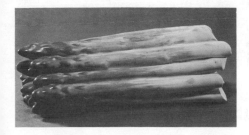

Figure 74. Box in the Form of a
Bunch of Asparagus. France, Sceaux
(ca. 1765). Faience. The Cleveland
Museum of Art, The Norweb Collection.

7

The Enrichment

Few of the visual arts afford more diverse possibilities for the enrichment of surfaces and of forms than does the art of pottery, and few are the pots which in no way expound this potential. For whether fortuitous or deliberate, reticent or forthright, the textures and colors and patterns with which man has enriched his ceramics indicate that he, as well as nature, seems to abhor a vacuum. The primitive basket or coil-built pot, perhaps intended for the storage of grain or other foodstuffs, would have functioned equally well without woven-in patterns or slip decorations; present-day utilitarian wares, whether produced by the craftsman or by some automaton, are seldom without color or ornament, neither of which contributes to serviceability; and even the discreetly nude white porcelain dinnerware, for some reason reputed to afford a tone of sophistication, is not without its decorative quality, even though undecorated, in the sheen of its white glaze and the austerity of its surface.

Perhaps the terms "decoration" and "ornament" in themselves are misnomers, for both seem to imply a superficial or added element, which unfortunately is too often true. But if considered as important means within the creative vocabulary of the potter which enable him to incorporate ideas and vitality and richness within his work, the decorative techniques are far removed from the extraneous. Nor must decoration always be considered a definite, planned pattern or motif, for the simple encompassing of a form with a sheath of unmodulated glaze, beautiful in its own color and texture, can in itself be one of the loveliest and most subtle of decorative statements, just as the innate and unexploited texture of a coarse-grained clay can be a bold one.

Despite the wide range of the potter's decorative means, wide both in its possible techniques and in its ultimate effects, an objective division into three broad and comprehensive categories is possible. Many finished wares, however, indicate an overlapping or an involvement of several techniques. Such divisions of decorative possibilities are those which can be termed *fortuitous* and include the effects which are innate within materials or those produced by fire, independent of the potter's skills other than his vision to recognize and exploit them; the *fabricative*, those surface or form variations and textures which are not inherent in raw materials but rather which are incidental to the methods employed by the craftsman to shape those materials; and the *factitious,* not indicative of artificiality but rather of deliberation in producing an effect not innate in materials and methods. It is perhaps overly pedantic to attempt such a classification, but it poses a point from which a broad and important aspect of the ceramic arts can be surveyed.

Although fortuitous or uncontrolled effects are not a direct manifestation of the potter's creativity, they are neither always completely accidental nor beyond his control. Of importance are the colors and the textures of clays themselves, as they occur naturally or as they are blended together or with other materials to achieve desired tonalities or textures. The rich redness of common red clay and the soft speckle produced by iron "impurities" in grey-firing stoneware clays are innate, awaiting only the anticipation by the potter of their fired qualities. The whiteness and delicacy of fine porcelains and the color of those which are artificially stained, such as the basalt and jasper wares of Wedgwood, are more contrived, yet depend primarily upon a basic quality of material rather than upon the potter's manipulation of that quality for their ultimate decorative effect.

The range of the fortuitous extends from the raw clay stage through all processes to the ultimate firing, and it is within the latter that perhaps most occur. For it is always with hope that a potter places his unresolved wares within the kiln, with the anticipation that the fire might add its own creative touch. Such hope of the unexpected is perhaps more the mark of the modern artist-potter than of the traditional craftsman whose intent is one of functional pieces rather than one of creativity, but dull indeed must be the life of any potter who is so rational in his approach and so sure of his work's outcome that the unstacking of the kiln is a mundane affair. For the relatively uncontrolled speckling of stoneware bodies, the flash of color on unglazed surfaces where caressed by fire, the unpredictable yet hoped for running of glazes (but, equally hopefully, not *too* runny!) into rich areas and textures, are among the fortuitous effects. The range of materials, techniques, and equipment available today make such incidence of luck a bit more predictable and even controllable. Indeed, pottery effects are often the result of planned or controlled "accidents," yet the pottery spectrum is far richer because of the whims of the fire as well as of the whims of the firer.

An esthetic, and perhaps ethical, point is often raised concerning the validity of accepting as works of art those pots which are beautiful or noteworthy because of an accident or another unpredicted element. Can a potter, for instance, logically assume credit for a glaze which he had intended to be a pale copper blue, but which, due to his inexperience in the firing of the kiln or a chance shift in its gas input, develops a beautifully rich copper red color? It remains one of those fascinating questions which, hopefully, will remain unresolved; but it seems valid to consider that for the few such moments of good fortune any potter experiences, he has many more which are less happy, and it is his decision which remains paramount in determining the value of these effects.

The writer once accidentally bashed in the side of a freshly thrown pot as it was being eased from the wheel, and rather than try to correct it or return it to the clay bin, he simply saw the distorted piece through to a conclusion. It is now in the permanent collection of a major museum, perhaps a better pot because it was completed with a sense of abandon rather than of overdevotion. And no one seems to have questioned its validity, particularly not the potter!

More controlled than the fortuitous, and yet an organic element in pottery, are those effects which can be termed fabricative—the surface and form variations which are not inherent in the raw materials but rather in the way in which wares are formed. These are the marks of the potter's fingers or tools, impressed during the shaping of the wares from shapeless clay, during cutting or carving it to its final form and surface, or the burnishing often used by primitive potters to impact unglazed surfaces leaving a slightly dappled, glossy finish. Such surfaces are neither the inherent fortuities of the clay nor are they superficially applied finishes, but are rather the "birthmarks" of the pot. Somehow the pot which retains the marks of its forming seems a lively one; somehow the one which has its fabrication masked by the removal of all such marks or by their superficial addition to falsify a forming technique can seem vapid. Examples of such artifice are the often crudely removed mold lines of slip-cast pieces, the messy sponging of coil-built forms to make them appear "smooth," and the artificial tooling or trimming of wares on the potter's wheel to make them seem thrown.

Such evidence of fabrication is often far more than decorative, for it can afford a manifest statement of a potter's intent. This has become particularly evident in the recent direction of the ceramic arts in the United States, for the retention of the creative process seems a dominant trait in the current style or trend in ceramics, whether pottery or sculpture. This is hardly an innovation, however, for many ceramics far removed in time from the present day still bear the feeling of soft, malleable clay, unaffectedly and directly fashioned.

In many instances, this fabricative quality is an obvious and animated indication of how the piece was formed: the freshness of a slab of clay, rolled, cut, bent, or applied to another clay surface; the plastic ooze of a fat coil, rolled, bent, and then pressed, pinched, or paddled into place; the freedom of an off-round pot, spiralled from a clay lump in a rhythm measured by taut marks of fingers, obviously thrown on a revolving wheel yet somehow not inhibited by the stuffy requirement that all shapes so executed be round. Glazes and colored slips are applied with a vigor and freedom, often over partial surfaces rather than over entire forms; the variations of firing in the kiln are anticipated rather than avoided. Such qualities are surely far more than surface ornament, for they are an organic and inseparable part of a pot's fabric, and of its very essence.

Any marked division would be arbitrary between those decorative qualities which are inherent in the forming of wares and those which are deliberately applied, if any such delineation is at all necessary or of any great significance, for often the simplest rhythms of the craftsman working his clay are left indelibly in that clay and appear almost calculated. But factitious ornament, playing across pottery surfaces in a wide compass of textures, colors, patterns, and motifs, assures pottery of its traditional place in the hierarchy of the decorative arts. These are the definite and intentional enrichments: tactile when stamped or pressed or carved or modelled in clay; rich and earthy in tonality when applied with colored slips or cut through layers of such slips in energetic or gossamer lines; vivid in the spectrum made possible by underglaze and overglaze pigments, by glazes, and by overglaze enamels; often pictorial when pottery surfaces are used as a foil for subject matter more illustrative than decorative; and iridescent or glittering when finished with superficial coatings of metals, far removed from that "claylike" perhaps too often cited as mandatory in integral potting, yet surely within its decorative potential.

As pottery emerges from the raw and amorphous clay materials and progresses toward an ultimate fired entity, it passes through stages during many of which quite different decorative techniques may be realized. Soft clay yields to manipulations quite impossible if the same clay dried partially to the leather-hard stage; leather-hard surfaces may be readily carved or decorated with clay slips, but if permitted to become bone-dry, would be rather resistant to the carving tool or to the adherence of most slips; biscuit-fired wares present wide possibilities for glaze and other color treatments difficult on pieces at other stages; and after a glaze has been fused into place, it still affords a surface for overglaze pigments or metallic lusters. So specific are these many techniques and so intrinsic their effects that a descriptive sequence suggests itself, briefly describing the methods and illustrating their results, hopefully surveying a vast creative aspect of pottery and at the same time affording some insight into the richness of the ceramic tradition.

Decoration may begin as most pots are begun, with soft and plastic clay, and some even begin with liquid clay, as are the agate wares of variegated patterns produced by pouring casting slips of different colors into molds simultaneously. Such pieces are all too readily available in the tourist traps of the American Southwest, reputedly capturing something of desert sands and sunsets but actually reflecting rather tawdry American taste. Similar effects are possible through the coarse blending of masses of various colored plastic clays and cutting the mass into slabs or throwing it on the wheel, but unless accomplished very directly, such wares are apt to appear smeary.

Many of the decorative treatments which involve the manipulation of clay into formal patterns or into individual motifs are tactile in structure, for they can actually be felt and depend upon variation in texture and surface plane rather than upon color. Colored slips and glazes, however, often serve to dramatize such treatment (Fig. 50). Fabricative surfaces are often the only such textural factor, and rich indeed they can be, whether retaining only the consistent rhythm of forming (Fig. 75), or showing conscious variation (Fig. 76). This is evident on many primitive pots, with the coils on some joined together in a plastic movement of clay from one coil into the adjacent, serving to unite the

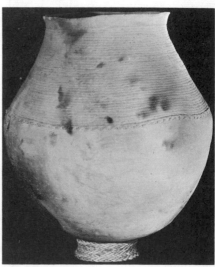

Figure 75. Cooking Pot. New Mexico (*ca.* A.D. 1100–1250). 12½″ h., 14″ d. Courtesy of The School of American Research, Indian Arts Fund Collection.

Figure 76. Coil-necked Cooking Pot. Pitoche type, New Mexico (*ca.* A.D. 1100–1250). 16¾″ h., 15″ d. Courtesy of The School of American Research, Indian Arts Fund Collection.

coils in a physical and structural way, and also to afford a richly plastic surface texture. On others, the coils have been smoothed onto a sheer surface, often burnished, after becoming leather-hard, to a more compact and serviceable wall and at the same time assuming a lovely dappled sheen.

The mark left by the potter's fingers as they shape his work on the revolving wheel can be a decoration within itself, and frequently potters have gently eased or briskly altered their freshly thrown, soft forms in a way which accents thrown textures (Figs. 61, 64). Clay slabs joined by a rhythmic thumbing or tooling can retain this rich mark of their assembly.

While wares are leather-hard or half-dry, it is often difficult for a potter to resist the addition of plastic embellishment, for in this stage pottery walls yield easily to a sharp metal cutting tool or softly to one of wood, yet they are firm enough to withstand the pressure of such instruments without any great distortion of gross forms. Such decorations may be incised, cut, or combed into the surface (Fig. 80), or may be excised by the removal of the background clay to leave a pattern standing in low relief. The sides of a form may be deliberately planed or shaved to produce a new and rather soft-sided geometric volume, retaining, however, the round basis of the original (Fig. 56). Additions to the surface are possible through the use of dabs, coils, or pancakes of clay, and such may be modelled or worked to achieve an almost relief sculpture (Fig. 37). Such appliqués may be formed in molds and reproduced in any number, a method termed "sprigged-on" decoration which has been widely used, perhaps most notably on the blue and white, and other colored Wedgwood wares (Fig. 82).

Although such applied motifs need not involve any change in the color of the basic piece, it is entirely possible to add units in clays of contrasting colors, as on the aforementioned Wedgwood. Such contrast, however, is usually most successful when left to a final coating of glaze to accent the surface variation and yet unify the pot's surface tonality. A change of color along with a change of surface plane, concurrent when a clay of a different color is applied, often can give the appearance of ornament superficially applied rather than of an organic part of the surface.

The use of clays of contrasting colors, however, is one of the most widely used of all decorative methods. Slip painting, the application of liquid clay pigments, is perhaps found on more wares than any other decorative technique. This is logical and natural, for colored earths are to be found abundantly and have been used on many surfaces other than those of pottery, as they have been on cave walls and on the human body.

Figure 77. Jug. Iran (tenth century). Almost white-grey. Very thin and light in weight. Dinted irregularly. Foot hollowed. No trace of glaze. 6¾" h. The Cleveland Museum of Art, Purchase from the Worcester R. Warner Fund.

Figure 78. Urn (*kame*). Japan, mid-Jomon Period (*ca.* 2000 B.C.). Terra cotta, 15½" h. The Cleveland Museum of Art, John L. Severance Fund.

Figure 79. Jar and Cover on Pierced Pedestal. Korea, Old Silla Dynasty (57 B.C.–A.D. 668). Stoneware, 8½" h. The John R. Fox Collection of Korean Ceramics, Syracuse University. Photograph courtesy of Syracuse University.

Plastic variation of pottery surfaces. See also Figures 7, 8, 34, 45, 57, 59, 64.

Figure 80. Bowl, Northern Celadon Ware. China, Northern Sung Dynasty (A.D. 960–1127). Porcelain, 8¼″ d. The Cleveland Museum of Art, The Fanny Tewksbury King Collection.

Figure 81. Jug. Germany (1574). White stoneware, 13⅝″ h. Courtesy of The Art Institute of Chicago.

Figure 82. Vase. England, Wedgwood (1792). Jasper, tricolor. One of a pair. Courtesy of The Art Institute of Chicago.

Slip decoration differs from the aforementioned plastic surface techniques in that there is little or no actual tactile alteration of surfaces when slip is painted on, and the effect is dependent upon the contrast of colors or values alone. What tactile variations occur seem secondary to the color change, such as the slightly raised surface of the slip areas, the marks of uneven deposition by brush, or the more raised form of the slip where it is trailed rather than painted on (Figs. 90 and 93). Slip decorations are to be found on so many early wares that it is difficult to cite any one piece as being archetypical or outstanding, so handsome are many of them. Specific examples which might be pointed out are those of the American Indian (Fig. 88), the rich and colorful wares of pre-Columbian Central and South America (Figs. 67 and 71), and those of the Mediterranean cultures (Fig. 83). It is of importance to note that all such early wares are without a covering of glaze.

In the above types, the slip itself is the positive note of decoration, with the pottery surface serving as a background. In the technique of sgraffito,[1] the slip coating comprises a background through which the decoration is cut or carved to reveal a pattern in the color of the underlying body. Such may be most delicate and linear in manner, which would be quite difficult if the slip were the positive element in the decoration. Sgraffito, however, is not limited to such linear treatment, for entire areas may be thus carved away in bold patterns. Lines may also be incised before the application of slip, and the slip washed over the lines or within the areas defined (Fig. 89). Another variation is to be found in certain Tz'u Chou types of Sung China, on which layers of slip glaze have been applied and cut through, the slip fusing into glazes of lustrous browns and blacks, and thus affording contrast in both color and texture to the stony quality of the scratched away and hence unglazed areas. On other pieces, the entire surface has been coated with a transparent glaze, covering both slip and carved areas, with the glaze often flowing together with the underlying slip into a soft, feathery texture (Fig. 96). It is difficult to find ceramics of any epoch which have more vigor and bite in their decoration than that of some of these Sung monuments, and indeed their beauty and decisiveness of line have few peers in the graphic arts in any medium.

The use of glazes, colored or colorless, to cover slips broadens the palette limited to the earthy range in unglazed primitive wares. Among the jewels of pottery are some wares of the Near East, on which layers of dark slip have been applied and scratched through, and the entire surface lavished with a glowing, transparent blue-green, copper-bearing glaze. The effect is a pattern of black areas where the glaze lies over the dark slip; brilliantly colored where it lies over the lighter-toned clay. Similar are the pieces in which the pattern has been painted in dark underglaze pigments rather than with slip.

Slip decorations are usually visual rather than tactile unless a pot's surface has been strongly cut by sgraffito. Patterns may be executed by methods which produce a definite "raised" appearance. Such is slip trailing, by which a linear pattern is developed by squeezing or forcing liquid clay through a small aperture in a raised line resembling a strand of graphic "spaghetti" (Fig. 90). The line may be single if the tool has but one opening, or may consist of a number of parallel lines if it has more than one opening. Traditionally, the slip-trailing tool has been a hollow pottery vessel with one or more poultry quills delivering the fluid slip, but modern ingenuity has made possible a number of tools not actually intended for such a purpose but which serve quite well, such as glass tubes, balloons, ear syringes, and catsup and mustard dispensers of flexible plastic. Even toy plastic baby bottles work beautifully.

The trailed slip may be of the same clay as the ware being decorated and thus produce a raised line of the same color as the ware, accented by the light it catches and the shadow it casts. When covered by glazes, such lines often break into a rich color accent as the glaze pulls away from them during firing; or they may be used as retaining walls similar to the cloisonné technique of the enamelists, with glazes of various colors flooded into them. Or such lines may be of colors different from the clay of the pot and may be covered by transparent glazes as in the slip wares of England and colonial America (Fig. 90). The slip may be manipulated while still liquid directly after its application to produce marbled or feathered patterns.

A most liquid and painterly handling of the slip technique is to be found on the bucolic salt-glazed wares of this country. To decorate such jugs and crocks, a small quantity of cobalt is added to clay slip, and this liquid is painted or trailed on the pots in an amazing fantasy of bird and animal and floral motifs, and often indicates with great flourish the gallon capacity of a jug. In the kiln, the slip assumes the blue typical of cobalt, and the body affords a sympathetic background, grey or tan, with an orange peel-textured glaze. This sturdy and homely family of wares is strong evidence of the urge of man to enrich the mundane articles of his daily life, and seldom has it been accomplished more spontaneously or beautifully (Fig. 92).

Many works by contemporary artist-potters incorporate dark colored slip decoration covered by thick and viscous mat glazes, usually white in color. Such slips are usually high in iron content, burning to browns or blacks, and dramatically or subtley mixing with the covering glaze to produce textures of speckled richness. Often no deliberate pattern

Decorated Unglazed Wares

Unglazed wares decorated with colored slips or other earthy pigments. Several incorporate sharply incised lines, done before or after the application of the pigment.

Figure 83. Amphora. Greece, Mycenean (fifteenth century B.C.). Painted in red, 15 15/16″ h. The Toledo Museum of Art, gift of Edward Drummond Libbey.

Figure 84. Alabastron (ointment vase). Greece, Corinthian (seventh century B.C.). 6½″ h. The Toledo Museum of Art.

Figure 85. Amphora in Geometric Style. Greece, Attica (eighth century B.C.). The Toledo Museum of Art.

Figure 86. White-ground Lekythos. Ascribed to Douris. Greece, Attica (ca. 500–490 B.C.). The Cleveland Museum of Art, purchase, Leonard C. Hanna, Jr., Bequest.

Figure 87. Pottery Swan. Greece, Corinthian (found in Vulci) (sixth century B.C.). The Toledo Museum of Art, gift of Edward Drummond Libbey.

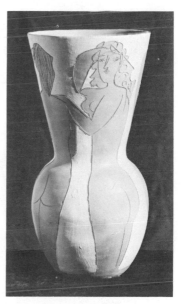

Figure 88. Pueblo Storage Jar. San Ildefanso, New Mexico (ca. 1880–1900). 25″ h., 22″ d. Courtesy of The School of American Research, Indian Arts Fund Collection.

Figure 89. Vase. Pablo Picasso. France (1950). Slip-painted earthenware, 25⅞″ h. The Toledo Museum of Art.

Figure 90. Dish, "Pelican in Her Piety." Attributed to Ralph Simpson, Staffordshire, England (1690). Slip-trailed decoration of a pelican feeding her young with her blood, a symbol of Christ shedding his blood. Border with heads of William II and his initials. 18¼" d. Courtesy of The Art Institute of Chicago.

Figure 91. Slipware Pie Dish. United States, Pennsylvania German (1840). Sgraffito decoration through white slip, with touches of coloring oxides. Courtesy of The Art Institute of Chicago.

Figure 92. Salt-glazed Stoneware Jug. United States (nineteenth century). Slip decoration in cobalt blue, 13" h. Collection of the author.

Glazed, Slip-Decorated Wares.

Figure 93. Jar with Handles and Slip Decoration: Tz'u Chou Ware. China, Northern Sung Dynasty (960–1127). Stoneware, 4½" h. The Cleveland Museum of Art, gift of Dr. and Mrs. Sherman E. Lee.

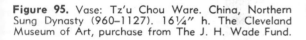

Figure 94. Dish with Design of Three Wild Geese in Flight: Nezumi Shino Ware. Japan, Monoyama Period (*ca.* 1600). White body, decoration scratched through red clay slip, greyish-white feldspathic glaze, 6½" d. The Cleveland Museum of Art, Mrs. A. Dean Perry Collection.

Figure 95. Vase: Tz'u Chou Ware. China, Northern Sung Dynasty (960–1127). 16¼" h. The Cleveland Museum of Art, purchase from The J. H. Wade Fund.

Figure 96. Vase with Peony Decoration. China, Sung Dynasty (960–1278). 11⅞" h. The Cleveland Museum of Art, gift of William G. Mather.

is attempted, with even or uneven applications of slip and glaze for-
tuitously intermingling as they fuse.

Similar in technique to slips but different in materials is underglaze, for this is painted onto the surface of wares, usually in the green
or biscuit stage, and as the name implies, is covered by glaze. The
pigments themselves are chemically compounded rather than naturally
occurring as are most slips. They usually consist of a number of materials, sintered or prefused and subsequently ground to a fine powder,
and are relatively nonfusible. The wares on which they are painted are
usually white or nearly white, giving a background against which the
colors are obvious. The glaze is transparent to make the painting visible,
although a semitransparent glaze can give a soft or muted quality. The
color range extends almost across the painter's palette in a vast array
of beautiful and of garish hues. The technique has been beautifully
used, as on the Ming Dynasty underglaze blue plate shown in Figure
97, on which the brushwork of the painting is of an outstanding and

Figure 97. Porcelain Dish.
China, Southern Fukien Prov-
ince, Ming Dynasty (late sixteenth–early seventeenth century). White porcelain, decoration in underglaze blue,
18⅝" d. The Cleveland Mu-
seum of Art, gift of Osborne
and Victor Hague.

lyric richness, but it has also been horribly misused, as evidenced by
the untold grosses of cheap and gaudy trivia to be found in department
and hardware stores, and particularly in "gift shoppes." And the claim
stamped on the bottoms of many such pieces that they are "hand-painted
underglaze" is seldom proof of merit.

It is difficult to program a definite place in the theoretical production sequence of pottery for the means which poses perhaps the greatest

decorative potential of all: glaze. Some glazes are applied to wares in the leather-hard stage, as are the slip glazes; to pieces which are bone-dry, with the pot and its final coating of glaze fired but once and simultaneously; most frequently to low-fired and absorbent biscuit wares whose porosity makes application less of a mechanical problem; to wares which have been given a high initial firing and are nonporous, such as china; or to those which have already had a glaze fused to their surface and are given a subsequent firing at a lower temperature than the preceding.

But such considerations seem insignificant in relation to the importance of this thin layer of glassy material, fused onto ceramic surfaces for functional or esthetic purposes, as a creative means, for the colors and textures of glazes pose almost limitless possibilities. Colors range from the most brilliant, as in the shimmering and deep copper alkaline blues of some Near Eastern wares, to the velvet subtleness of some of Sung China; from the slick smoothness of contemporary tablewares to the stony grittiness of some stoneware surfaces. Textures of glazes may be smooth and flowing, as if they caressed pottery surfaces while flowing across them in the fire, or stubbornly staying in place, often barely fused. The methods by which glazes are applied or are combined with each other are important factors, for a glaze can be quite different when brushed onto a pot than when poured over it, and such procedural techniques are important to the potter. On the contrary, many contemporary potters disavow the importance of glaze, and feeling that it is no end in itself, use it with reticence or reduce its emphasis to a minimum in favor of more obvious dependence upon clay and structural surface qualities.

Glaze belongs to the large system of man-produced silicates known as glasses. Silica by itself can be melted into a glassy state at a temperature of about 3100 degrees Fahrenheit, but it would be difficult to find a practical pottery body which could withstand such heat. The fusion point of the silica in glazes is lowered by combination with materials termed fluxes or fluxing agents, sometimes to the degree that the glaze will develop at a very low red heat. Such glazes may be mere washes of white lead or galena coated over a pottery surface, and what silica is present in the fired glaze has been absorbed from the underlying clay. Glazes of this type, found on wares such as many produced in Mexico, are soft and nondurable, easily chipped, and all too readily soluble in weak acids such as vinegar. But fluxing agents, whether they produce glasses at high or low temperatures, also contribute certain chemical and physical properties to glazes and affect their colors and their surface textures. Thus a glaze whose chief flux is an alkali such as soda or potash gives a brilliant turquoise blue when copper compounds are added as coloring agents; the same coloring agent will result in a brilliant bottle green in a glass in which lead is the chief melting agent.

Although glazes can be described under many systems and by many terms, such descriptions can be so varied that they are easily confused. Salt glaze, for instance, implying a method and a type, is formed when salt is thrown into the incandescent atmosphere of a kiln and is decomposed. The resulting sodium vapors combine with the silica present in the wares being fired to produce a glassy coating. A slip glaze actually describes the raw material used as a glaze and its method of application to pottery, but a copper blue is a specific color derived from a specific agent. Such a list of nominal terms might be extended to great length, yet few terms would bear within themselves an objective description enlightening to the person who is nonconversant with ceramic terms. It is possible, however, to describe any particular glaze in a few words indicative of fired properties rather than of chemical composition or other idiosyncrasies which are of little interest other than technical.

Foremost among such terms are those which describe the surface quality of a glaze and its capacity to reflect or disseminate light waves. A glass which is shiny and can reflect an image from its surface is termed bright; one which is dull and produces no reflections and little highlight is mat.[2] There are many stages between these two, which can be described as semibright, semimat, or semiglossy, but to attempt to objectively establish a definite scale of such degrees would be difficult and meaningless.

Bright glazes might be compared with the surface of a sheet of glass or of tranquil water, shiny and smooth, capable of reflecting an image from their surfaces. Mat glazes are rough rather than smooth, similar to a sheet of sandpaper whose surface consists of tiny particles, none of which is large enough to reflect a total image but which, in contrast to a bright glaze, scatters light waves which strike it.

Mat glazes are of many types, two of which are quite basic. One consists of particles not carried high enough in temperature to achieve a complete melt, similar to slushy snow which, when the big thaw comes, can melt to a liquid. Such glazes have a rather dry quality and show any inconsistencies or subtleties of application by brushing or pouring as they do not move or flow during firing. The mat glazes of the other basic type, the crystalline mat, have been carried to a liquid melt, and crystallization occurs during cooling, resulting in an interlocking structure of microscopic forms, similar on an infinitely smaller scale to the touch of Jack Frost on the windowpane. Such mat glazes often flow while liquid in the kiln, and some may show an almost violent surge which solidifies upon cooling. These effects are as dependent upon firing

Figure 98. Thrown Porcelain Bottle. Marc Hansen. Transparent green glaze with blue-green crystals, 12½" h. Photograph courtesy of the artist.

and cooling rates as they are upon chemical composition. Thus a glaze cooled rapidly may be quite bright, while the same glaze cooled slowly may definitely mat when crystals have had time to grow. Under especially controlled firing conditions, crystals may be grown in very fluid glazes which appear as feather or plant forms suspended in the glassy mix, or as floating islands of rich and glowing color (Fig. 98).

Coordinate with its surface quality is a glaze's capacity to transmit or deflect light waves as a function of its inner structure as well as of its surface, a property indicated in terms of transparency or opacity. A transparent glaze, like a transparent sheet of window glass, permits an almost complete penetration of light waves. Some, however, are reflected from the surface, others selectively from the underlying clay body, making apparent the color of that body and that of any slip or underglaze decoration involved.

In contrast, an opaque glaze does not permit penetration by light waves, but rather reflects them before they reach the clay body. It is selective absorption of light rays which is responsible for colors both in opaque and transparent glazes. Opacity may be due to undissolved particles suspended in the glass, such as tin oxide which produces the typical opaque tin white enamels, or crystals which develop in mat glazes during cooling. Opacity is generally quite complete in a heavy mat glaze; bright glazes may be either transparent or opaque. This relationship is often quite confusing, but a simple comparison might prove clarifying: water is bright and transparent (with no consideration of the refraction or bending of light rays as they pass through it); milk is bright and opaque, the opacity the result of tiny particles of fats and other solids suspended in its water base; snow is mat and opaque, chemically identical to the water in the first comparison above, but crystallized. And as between transparent and opaque glazes, there are many degrees of variation between bright and mat, described as semi-bright or semimat.

Whether glazes are bright or mat, transparent or opaque, few can completely mask the color of the bodies over which they are applied. Often the final quality of the fired glaze is not as dependent upon the glaze itself as it is upon its thickness of application, for a thin layer of an opaque, white glaze over a dark clay body can have the same effect as does a transparent glaze, and a thin coating of a white mat glaze can lack the typical mat glaze richness and appear dry and without character. When it is attempted to completely hide the body tonality with an opaque glaze, the result is often superficial and "painted," as on many commercial wares, particularly those of the "pastel" or "rainbow" strata. Some glazes, however, which are completely opaque and through which the body is not apparent can be so beautiful and rich in their own substance that the clay becomes rather insignificant in the total statement of the piece.

Of parallel importance to the texture and the opacity of glazes is the element of color, and the possibilities of glaze color are as limitless as are those inherent in the spread of pigments across the painter's palette. Combined with the various other decorative means at the potter's command, colored glazes become one of the most lively factors within the ceramic discipline. The spectrum is wide, ranging from the subdued earth colors, the rich blacks and countless browns, the glowing copper and cobalt blues, to the brilliant yellows of chrome and the reds of chrome and selenium. The tradition of pottery, however, seems to have largely confined itself within a range limited to the earthy tonalities, and for this contemporary pottery has often been criticized. At the present time, however, American studio potters seem to be emerging from the subtley colored stoneware rut in which they have been submerged, and the splash of color which has so often played across the ceramic scene is again becoming apparent.

Although a glaze may in itself be colorless, it can appear to have a color because of that of the body which it covers or that of an undercoat of slip. A rich, iron-bearing brown or reddish body, for instance, might be covered with a colorless transparent glaze, colorless but lustrous brown in appearance, and appear darker than the body, for it seems to "moisten" the clay underneath, just as a piece of fabric may seem darker and richer when wet than when dry. Whether or not an opaque, white glaze is colorless or colored can be a matter of debate, but when such a glaze "picks up" a tonality or speckled texture from the pot's body, the result can be rich and colorful. This effect has been used on a good portion of the work produced by studio potters since the awakening of interest in high-fire wares, and is characteristic of perhaps too much of the stoneware being produced today.

Color in glazes is accomplished by the mixing or dissolving in the glass of metallic compounds. Some seem to go readily into the glassy melt, others probably remain suspended in a colloidal or crystalline state. Many physical and chemical factors enter into the potential of any coloring agent, factors which become quite complex. In summation they include the inherent color of any metal (blue, for instance, is typical of cobalt; copper usually produces green or blue-green); the chemical composition of the glass, with many coloring agents producing entirely different hues when introduced into a lead glaze or into an alkaline; the firing temperature, with a range that becomes more narrow as the higher temperatures are approached; kiln atmosphere; various color influencers which may be present in the glaze or glazes on pots surrounding any given one in the kiln; and of notable importance, the mere thickness of the application of the glaze itself, for a thin or stringent layer has little chance to exhibit its color, but where it has been applied in a sufficient thickness, it builds up to good effect; the pulling away from the sharp edges of pottery forms or from the textures of surface variations and the massing together as it pools within depressions often evince a rich interplay of clay and its glaze (Fig. 80).

Particular colors or color effects resulting from the use of particular coloring agents are so often unique to that agent that many of the names assigned to pottery types are often derived from that agent or signify a color produced by it. Typical are Delft or cobalt blue, copper blue, copper red and its many hybrids such as peach bloom and oxblood (sang-de-boeuf), chrome green, chrome red, chrome yellow, antimony yellow, and a paint box full of others.

Beautiful glazes, however, are not beautiful pottery, for they are not entities within themselves, and even the most disciplined of technical research or the most sophisticated of formulas do not mean more beautiful pottery. Nor are glazes a mask, for the most exotic of glazes cannot evoke a significant form from one which is basically insipid. Conversely, some shapes might well be left unglazed rather than given a distracting or unsympathetic finish. As a potter weighs the considerations of whether or not to glaze a piece, of what glaze to select to manifest his ideas, and of the objective relationship of glaze and pot, he is also faced with the inherencies of glaze as a decorative means within itself.

One of the simplest, and perhaps at the present time one of the most often overlooked, decorative manipulations of glaze is the use of a single glaze to embellish a simple, unmodulated form, with the final effect dependent upon the color and texture of the glaze as they define and enhance the form. Such treatment is found on some works which rank among the most austere and timeless in the realm of pottery, for they depend upon no local or historical style nor upon any decorative fad or whim, but rather upon a relationship of form and color alone. Often such simple pieces are cited as being copies of Oriental wares or overly influenced by them, but perhaps they simply share a principle which is universal rather than unique to any one epoch, a universal which has few peers in the elegance with which it has been incorporated in certain Chinese celadons and monochrome enamels (Fig. 99). Some of the Chinese forms, of course, are unique to their own epoch, and these are the forms which have been imitated or adapted rather than their glaze-form relationship.

A more factitious use may be made of a single glaze by applying it in restricted areas rather than to a total form, establishing definite motifs, happy splashes, or controlled patterns, in all of which the clay surface affords a foil for a contrasting color or texture of a glaze (Fig. 100).

More dramatic effects are presented by the combination of several glazes on a single piece, such as contrasting glazes on inner and outer surfaces, or the inner or outer surfaces alone when utilitarian considerations are not involved. The use of different glazes, perhaps one dark and one white, applied over one another across the entire surface or in a prescribed pattern (Fig. 101) is a fascinating device of many contemporary potters; for no matter how careful and controlled the application of the component glazes, the opening of the kiln after firing often reveals many surprises of blotching, spotting, or otherwise intermixing of colors and textures.

As well as serving by itself or in combination with others to enrich a pottery surface, a glaze can provide the background on which formal decoration is applied, as in the glaze painting mentioned above. Handsome examples of this approach are the majolica wares of Spain and Renaissance Italy. Majolica is fascinating historically, the technique[3] being of Near Eastern origin and brought to Spain during the eighth to fifteenth centuries with the Islamic sweep across the North of Africa. Swept along were not only the method but also stylistic motifs, such as the arabesque, and the urge to totally enrich all surfaces as those so resplendent on many Near Eastern wares and upon the buildings of Moorish Spain in a gay flourish of architectural tile.

Involved is the application of an opaque white glaze or tin enamel to the wares, and the application over this coating, before its firing, of a decoration, although in many instances the decoration might well be called illustration, so pictorial they become. The glaze and its decoration are fired simultaneously, with the decoration thus partially fusing or sinking into the glaze. On some wares, a final coating of transparent glaze "sandwiches" the decoration between its enamel base and a clear, covering layer.

Tonally, the wares are brilliant and sparkling in color, with a predominance of cobalt blue, antimony yellow, copper green, and manganese violet. Often touches of soluble salts of the coloring metals produce a soft and fuzzy texture, different from the usual crisp and

Figure 99. Apple-green Gallipot. China, Ch'ing Dynasty (1644–1912). White porcelain, overglazed with enamel following the initial firing, and refired at a lower temperature. The crackle pattern is the result of a higher degree of contraction of the glaze than the body upon cooling, producing the mesh or tiny cracks. Courtesy of The Art Institute of Chicago.

Figure 100. Stoneware Bottle. The author. Pinkish-tan body, white mat glaze. The resist pattern is produced by brushing the surface of the pot with melted wax. When the piece is dipped section by section into glaze, the glaze does not adhere to the waxed areas. 10" h.

Glaze as Enrichment

Wares incorporating a simple glazed surface and dependent upon the color and texture of the glaze itself; a pattern of glaze against the background of the clay body; and patterns of glaze against glaze backgrounds.

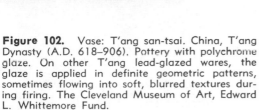

Figure 101. Stoneware Vase. Maija Grotell (1948). A large, globular shape, decorated with white and grey glazes. 13" h. The Toledo Museum of Art.

Figure 102. Vase: T'ang san-tsai. China, T'ang Dynasty (A.D. 618–906). Pottery with polychrome glaze. On other T'ang lead-glazed wares, the glaze is applied in definite geometric patterns, sometimes flowing into soft, blurred textures during firing. The Cleveland Museum of Art, Edward L. Whittemore Fund.

direct touch of nonsoluble pigments. The Spanish wares vary in form, and typical are the cylindrical apothecary (drug) jar and conventional jars and bowls. In rich array across these surfaces parade delightful birds and animals, beautifully and spontaneously drawn portraits (Fig. 104), fish, and plant motifs, most typical of which is the oak leaf (Fig. 103). All show a rather obvious Near Eastern stylistic flourish, a flourish which is even evident on contemporary Mexican pottery, indicative of the wanderlust of techniques and styles and their diffusion into the arts of their hosts.

The majolica of Renaissance Italy strongly suggests its Spanish and Near Eastern ancestry, but suffered at the hands of painters when pottery became the background for painting rather than a total shape to be enriched. Many potters are apt to squirm at the visual destruction of a plate by the application of the Renaissance investigation of the laws of visual perspective when that plate's concave surface is punctured with vast three-dimensional vistas. Art historians, however, are apt to wax eloquent at this same accomplishment.

Whereas majolica painting is applied over the unfired glaze and fired into its surface, other techniques involve decoration over a glaze after its firing, with the pigment fused onto the glaze rather than into it. Such are overglaze painting and decals, enamels which cover an entire piece or which are applied in definite figures or patterns, lusters, and actual metals. The advantages of these procedures are several. As has been previously discussed, the higher the degree to which body and glaze are fired, the more durable the final product, but the higher the degree, the more limited the palette of colors. Thus a type of ware desired to be as strong in body and glaze as possible would not permit the use of a number of agents whose prime colors are stable only within a lower temperature range. Conversely, if wares were fired to merely the low temperatures at which such agents are stable, they would be physically weak and probably quite soft and porous.

The overglaze paints and enamels are in themselves fusible glazes or pigments, capable of melting at the low temperatures at which their component coloring agents are usable. Such are many of the Chinese monochromes of the Ch'ing period, on which enamels cover the entire surfaces of pieces with colors such as rich "apple-green" or yellow, or serve as a colored background for further enamel painting of definite subjects. Overglaze paints are also low-fusing colors, differing from underglaze pigments in that they are fusible, and are merely melted onto the surface of the already fired glaze, whereas the underglaze colors are relatively nonfusible and lie directly on the body and underneath the glaze. One simple means of differentiating between the two is to

Figure 103. Two-handled Oak Leaf Drug Pot. Italy, Florence (second quarter fifteenth century). Majolica, 11⅝" h. The Cleveland Museum of Art, purchase from the J. H. Wade Fund.

Figure 104. Bowl with Portrait. Spain, Paterna, Valencia. Majolica, 14½" d. The Cleveland Museum of Art, in memory of Mr. and Mrs. Henry Humphreys, gift of their daughter, Helen.

Figure 105. Covered Porcelain Jar. The author (1958). An adaptation of the majolica technique to high-temperature porcelain. Cobalt and iron pigments were brushed over the surface of the opaque, white mat glaze before firing. The Cleveland Museum of Art, Silver Jubilee Treasure Fund.

Majolica. See also Figure 41.

note whether or not there is any change in the surface quality of the decoration where light strikes it. If the glaze appears just as glossy over the area of decoration as it does over undecorated areas, the technique is most likely underglaze; if there is a dullness or change of light reflection, it is overglaze. A decoration which appears to be slightly raised, however, is not always overglaze, for often underglaze pigments are so heavily applied that they appear almost in shallow relief.

Some overglaze enamel patterns are applied so thickly that they stand above the pottery surface and are hardly the most stable of decoration, for the lack of fusion to any great degree to the underlying glaze frequently results in a lifting off of the raised material. Such wares, often with the raised enamel portions further "enriched" by gold, are among the gaudiest and cheapest of pottery types and are readily available to tourists in "Chinatowns" hoping to find a genuine Oriental piece of pottery.

On such pieces genuinely Oriental, however, are to be found some of the loveliest color and painting in all of ceramics (Fig. 106).

The technique of overglaze painting enjoyed a heyday in the post-Victorian era of this country, during which countless cocoa pots and cups, serving dishes, and vases were emblazoned with violets, pine cones and branches, roses and rosebuds, and butterflies. Although the technique has been languishing in the hands and in the electric kilns of china painters, it probably afforded the wellspring out of which the present-day interest in pottery arose, and it might well see a revival in the hands of potters looking for "new" flourishes.

An actual touch of metal over a glaze can be one of subtle richness or of flashy gaudiness, dependent upon the thickness and extent of application and, as is so true in all phases of a potter's work, upon his taste and imagination. A coating of metal, microscopic in thickness, gives little effect of the metallic but rather of an iridescent sheen or flash of color, much as a thin layer of oil on water. This is luster, and the pottery world is indeed richer for such resplendent wares produced in the Near East, Spain, and Italy. Some lusters are applied in definite motifs

Figure 106. Porcelain Vase. China, Ch'ing Dynasty, K'ang Hsi Era (1662–1722). So-called "Black Hawthorne." White, yellow, aubergine and blue-green on black ground, 27" h. The Toledo Museum of Art, gift of Edward Drummond Libbey.

over colored or colorless glazes, often appearing as iridescent and shift-
ing patterns. The luster wares of Moorish Spain are alive in their play of
light across glowing birds, fantastic animals, whimsical human figures,
and freely drawn geometric patterns. Italian majolica is often given a
final flourish of luster over entire surfaces rather than in definite patterns, and it is of interest to steal a peek at the reverse side of Italian
and Spanish pieces in museum showcases, for often the artist who
applied the overall coating of luster to the face of a bowl would let
his fancy play free on the reverse, and fantastic eagles, sprightly rabbits,
flamboyant coats of arms, or delicate patterns of units such as the fleur-
de-lis glow there.

Figure 107. Samarra Ware
Bowl. Iran (Hamadan) (tenth
century). Five medallions of rabbits painted in brown luster over
a white glaze, 8¾″ d. The Toledo Museum of Art, gift of
Edward Drummond Libbey.

The application of metals in coatings thick enough to manifest them
as metals rather than as the sheen of lusters is also executed in a final
low-temperature fire. The principal metals thus used are gold and
platinum in varying degrees of purity. There are gold-bearing coatings
so high in content of the precious metal that they are indicated in carats,
and often require a final burnishing after firing to achieve their ultimate
polish. Such techniques can add a touch of richness and elegance to
wares, but too often produce a gaudiness. Available are cups and saucers,
teapots and coffeepots, and large trays, covered partially or overall
with gold, which somehow appear rather less than elegant, particularly
when in combination with florid displays of underglaze and overglaze
trivia. Perhaps the most successful use of such metals is a reticent touch

confined to a simple band as on much fine china, where gold is subordinate within a total effect rather than dominant to the point of
garish overstatement.

Even after ultimate firing, ceramics can still be given a final touch
which is not fixed by fire. A pigment may be rubbed into a crackled
glaze to stain and thus emphasize that crackle pattern, or a natural
accumulation of grime can do the same; surfaces may be given a final
rubbing of pigment to enrich an otherwise drab or monotonous tonality
or to enliven surface modulations; and even the use of synthetics such
as the acrylic paints may provide color, as well as a finish more permanent than that of soft lead glazes which all too readily deteriorate
or separate from their hosts. Nor are such nonceramic touches new-
comers, for early unglazed wares still bear evidence of greasy materials
probably intended to seal their porous walls, and traces of unfired
pigments remain on classic Greek wares and on T'ang mortuary pieces.

It might be argued that such treatments are not fired and thus are
neither ceramic nor valid ceramic media. Not to be overlooked, however, is the validity of any means by which an artist may convey ideas
or develop new form, for it is through such flexibility of ideas and
materials that the potter adds his personal touch of enrichment to his
craft and to the world around him.

FOOTNOTES

[1]Variously spelled sgraffito, sgraffiato, graffito, graffiato, having the same root
as *graphic* and thus sharing the idea of linear writing or drawing.

[2]Variously spelled mat, matt, matte.

[3]"Faience" is perhaps a better term for the technique. See Glossary.

The Function

Surrounding the arts are many barricades, posed by tradition or self-imposed by artist, defined by media but enhanced by skill and imagination. Traditionally, pottery has been designated a craft, a minor art, a decorative art, and a utilitarian art, but for none of these, with the exception of the rather embarrassing "minor," need it offer an apology. For if the fine arts of painting, sculpture, and architecture have assumed their primacy through their image of man's creative spirit, the humble pots which manifest that same spirit might well rival them. If pottery is craft, there is also craft in the fine arts, perhaps with a varied degree of emphasis or importance, and often elided when the sloppy or inept is rationalized as "creative." If pottery is decorative, this too is true of architecture, as is evident in Gothic embellishment, in Baroque grandiosity, or on the sheer window-textured façades of many present-day structures, as well as in the "executive suite modern" paintings which discreetly, blatantly, or with obvious "taste" adorn the interiors of the latter, paintings in styles as clichéd and mannered as many traditional pottery concepts. If pottery is considered merely functional or utilitarian, it can serve not only mundane needs as actually does most architecture, but also serve with the arts of all media in a less tangible function, to be contemplated or enjoyed. Such barriers which have long defined the specific arts are becoming increasingly difficult to mark, for painting is often now more sculptural than painting in its traditional connotation, sculpture is more archetectonic than involved with the figurative or obvious subject, and pottery has been widening its nomenclature as it too departs from tradition to encompass a new identity as a plastic and creative form.

But persistent throughout all of pottery has been an undertone of utility, for no matter what technical factors are involved or what cultural or decorative facets engendered or reflected, most pottery implies a response to some basic human need. Such need may be simply practical, requiring vessels for the storage, preparation, and serving of foodstuffs; the need may be spiritual, calling for religious artifacts or for the mortuary articles associated with rites for the dead; it may be to afford embellishment to the human environment, for, as has previously been indicated, few are the ceramics which in no way involve the element of the decorative.

Yet mere satisfaction of such needs hardly implies esthetic merit, for many things which well serve their intended functions are indeed inane, and even these may be acclaimed by transient fad. The clichéd canon, that form follows function, may well be responsible for the sterility in concept and in result of many ceramic wares, as well as that of many other nonclay products, which flaunt the "good design" aura, bespeaking their inception on the drawing board and lacking the sympathetic involvement of the artist. Such wares frequently seem overdesigned rather than well-designed, and an example which might be cited is the pottery style with the "square" look, a look often found in pottery's counterpart in plastics. The square plate functions quite adequately, but the cup with its handle placed either along a flat side or radiating from a corner makes the usually simple act of drinking one of juggling or mopping up.

Such inadequacies are, however, not limited to mass-produced wares, for they occur all too often in the limited output of the artist-potter and equally often are accepted as innate in "hand-made" pottery. Pitchers and teapots which drip and gurgle rather than cleanly pour; cup handles which do not permit comfortable access of fingers or adequate grasp of the hand; flower vases which seep water; plates with rough clay surfaces which make eating, cutting, and dishwashing difficult, or those plates with mat glazes, lovely in color and in sheen but an audible horror when a knife or fork is screeched across them; planters which ignore the physiological requirements of living plants; lids on cookie jars and casseroles which are sloppy in their fit and which afford inadequate grip; "branch bottles" of huge and voluptuous form, handsome as sculpture and a joy to produce, but difficult to fill with water or to have their guest branches inserted through their tiny apertures— such are functional inadequacies often noted.

Although such functional considerations have little to do with the esthetic which separates the article which is merely manufactured from that which is beautifully crafted, adequate resolution of such practical involvements can lift pottery, as it can any craft form, above the prosaic. And it is indeed difficult to isolate the esthetic from the practical satisfactions of a utensil as mundane as a simple cup which is beautifully formed and beautiful in that form, which seems to invite itself to be picked up and used and enjoyed; of a pitcher, rich and jolly, satisfying in color and decoration, which feels comfortable and secure when gripped by its adequate and sculptural handle, and which pours cleanly without afterdrip; of a casserole which through its own color and texture enhances the food within it, which is safe to place in the oven without danger of breakage by heat shock, and whose lid can readily be removed; of the flower container or the planter, decoratively "functional" in the pleasures afforded even when empty, but somehow more satisfying when complemented by the flora, nature's unrivalled synthesis of beauty and function.

As nature, whether organic as in the flora or inorganic in the world it has sculptured, has been called the grand designer, nature conversely can hardly be labeled an artist, just as art is hardly a mere copy of nature, beautiful as it may be. But to this writer, it is the essence of craftsmanship, and of all art, that embodied within the final work is a feeling of the organic, of the plastic evolving ideas of the artist, and even when a work is presented as "finished," it still affords a springboard for conceptual changes within one's imagination. For craftsmanship seems far more than mere perfection of technique or of finish, and more the involvement of the artist with his medium and methods as he endows it with form and ideas and evokes from within it the colors and textures and mysteries latent there. Many man- and machine-made articles are technically quite perfect, yet far from indicative of creative capacity, and craftsmanship is not such superficial slickness imposed upon patient clay with sponge or scraper, for many dead pots have been so slaughtered. And a work indicative of perfect control of the means can appear too carefully done and too calculated. Conversely, complete freedom or abandon or sloppiness are hardly craftsmanship, for such can all too easily be accomplished under the guise of the uninhibitedly "creative," as has been apparent in certain transient art movements of recent years. Many seem eager to get aboard the bandwagon of a current fad and to jump off only to board another as one wanes and another looms, somehow lacking the personal impetus and involvement of the innovators of such directions.

Ultimately, pottery as an art thus remains a dialogue between the artist and his material. The potter endows a rather lifeless and formless and valueless material with forms, with his ideas, and with his values, while the material offers its attributes and its own peculiar beauty, and with the dialogue indicating that it might have paused at an apt moment or might have been carried yet further, but somehow was arrested while vital and alive, to be thus rather paradoxically frozen by fire.

And this, at least to me, is the fascination of the potter's craft, and of his art.

So every craftsman and workmaster that laboureth night and day, he who maketh graven seals, and by his continual diligence varieth the figure: He shall give his mind to the resemblance of the picture, and by his watching shall finish the work.

So doth the potter sitting at his work, turning the wheel about with his feet, who is always carefully set to his work, and maketh all of his work by number:

He fashioneth the clay with his arm, and boweth down his strength before his feet:

He shall give his mind to finish the glazing, and his watching to make clean the furnace.

All these trust to their hands, and every one is wise in his own art.

Without these a city is not built.

But they shall strengthen the state of the world, and their prayer shall be in the work of their craft, applying their soul, and searching in the law of the Most High.

Ecclesiasticus 38 : 28, 32-36, 39

suggested reading

The standard encyclopedias offer lengthy, well-illustrated sections under their headings of "Ceramics," "Pottery," or "Pottery and Porcelain," in addition to listings under specific types of ware.

The following publications, many intended primarily as textbooks, are suggested for their varied approaches to the philosophy and techniques of pottery:

LEACH, BERNARD, *A Potter's Book,* New York: Transatlantic Arts, Inc., 1967.

———, *A Potter's Work,* Great Britain: Evelyn, Adams & Mackay, Ltd., 1967.

NELSON, GLENN C., *Ceramics: A Potter's Handbook,* New York: Holt, Rinehart & Winston, Inc., 1966.

RHODES, DANIEL, *Clay and Glazes for the Potter,* Philadelphia: Chilton Book Company, 1967.

———, *Stoneware and Porcelain,* Philadelphia: Chilton Book Company, 1966.

SANDERS, HERBERT H., *The World of Japanese Ceramics,* Tokyo: Kodansha International, 1967.

WHITAKER, IRWIN, *Crafts and Craftsmen,* Dubuque, Iowa: Wm. C. Brown Company Publishers, 1967.

WILDENHAIN, MARGUERITE, *Pottery: Form and Expression.* New York: American Craftsmen's Council, 1959.

PERIODICALS

Ceramics Monthly, 4175 North High Street, Columbus, Ohio 43214.

Craft Horizons, The American Craftsmen's Council, 16 East 52nd Street, New York, New York 10022.

glossary
of descriptive pottery terms

AGATE WARE—Pottery of variegated or marbelized body color. It may be produced by shaping stratified masses of colored clays, or by the simultaneous pouring of slips of different colors into molds.

ASH GLAZE—A glaze whose chief flux is the residue left after the burning of organic materials such as wood or vegetation. Such glazes are usually of the high-fire feldspathic type, but are also possible within the lower temperature ranges.

BASALT—An unglazed, black, vitreous ware introduced by Wedgwood in 1768.

BELLEEK—A translucent ware of the soft-paste type, containing significant amounts of glass in the body and covered with a glaze of a "mother-of-pearl" quality. Irish.

BISCUIT, BISQUE—Unglazed, fired pottery. This may be a stage preliminary to the application of glaze and final firing, or a final stage in itself as in biscuit figurines or other unglazed wares.

BODY—The structural substance of pottery. It may be a single clay, a combination of clays, or a combination of clay or clays with other materials.

BONE CHINA—A white, translucent, usually quite thin body type, containing as its principal flux the ashes of burned bones, or calcium phosphate.

BRIGHT GLAZE—A glaze with a shiny or glossy surface.

CELADON—A soft green, blue-green, or olive-green glaze, produced by the reduction firing of iron-bearing glazes.

CHINA—A broad and generic term for tableware. Specifically, the ware is fired during its initial or biscuit firing to a vitreous or translucent state, and glazed and subsequently refired at a lower temperature.

CLOISONNÉ—A decorative treatment in which areas are defined by low retaining walls of clay (or of wire in metal enamels), and such areas filled with glaze.

COIL BUILDING, COIL-BUILT—Terms relative to the technique of pottery construction in which coils or ropes of plastic clay are the units of assembly. Such coils may or may not be apparent in the wall of the finished vessel.

COPPER RED—A red glaze color produced by the firing of copper-bearing glazes in a reducing atmosphere. Many Chinese wares of this glaze type have been assigned to specific categories, such as *flambé, sang-de-boef* (oxblood), peach-bloom, apple-red, and others.

CRACKLE GLAZE—A glaze which is marked by desired crazing in a definite pattern. See *crazing*.

CRAWLING—The separation of glaze from body during firing, with the glaze pulling together into "beads" surrounded by unglazed areas, or completely dropping from the ware. Sometimes crawling is used deliberately for its decorative effect.

CRAZING—Fissures or cracks in a fired glaze resulting from a greater contraction of glaze than body. Delayed crazing may occur for prolonged periods after firing.

CRYSTALLINE GLAZE—A glaze characterized by visible masses of crystal structure suspended within the glass.

DECAL, DECALCOMANIA—A decorative method widely used in commercial pottery production. Patterns are printed in underglaze or overglaze pigments on a paper backing, and transferred to biscuit or glazed surfaces.

DELFT—See *faience*.

DRY FOOT—A pottery base or foot ring which has not been glazed or from which glaze has been removed before firing.

EARTHENWARE—A term descriptive of a broad range of pottery characterized by opacity and a rather high degree of porosity or water absorption.

ENAMEL—A low-fusing glass or glaze applied to pottery surfaces after glaze firing to an initial high temperature and fired in place at a lower temperature. Enamel may be used to cover an entire surface as on K'ang-Hsi apple-green monochrome porcelains, or in definite patterns. Enamels are also used on metals.

ENGOBE—A slip or liquid clay usually applied over an entire surface rather than in restricted or decorative areas. Technically, there is little difference between engobe and slip, and the terms are often used interchangeably.

FAIENCE, MAJOLICA, DELFT—Pottery types which have been decorated by the application of pigment over the surface of an unfired tin enamel (opaque white glaze), and fired into the glaze surface. The difference between the three types is one of decorative style, and historical and geographic position rather than method. See index.

FELDSPATHIC GLAZES—High-fired glazes, used on stoneware and porcelain, with minerals of the feldspar type as chief components.

FIT—A glaze is said to "fit" a body when the degrees of thermal expansion and contraction of glaze and body are so in agreement that neither crazing nor shivering occurs.

FLAMBÉ—Reduced copper glazes, usually on porcelain, characterized by streaks of red and blue or violet.

FLAME WARE, FLAME PROOF—Pottery cooking ware which can safely be used over an open flame without cracking. Oven-proof does not imply flame-proof!

FRIT—A prefused material used in glazes, similar to powdered glass.

GLAZE—A glassy coating fused onto clay surfaces.

HARD PASTE—True, high-fired porcelain with kaolin and feldspar as the chief ingredients.

HIGH-FIRE, HIGH-FIRED—Relative terms designating an approximate firing range, usually pyrometric cones 8 to 15, *c.* 2300 to 3000 degrees F.

INCISED—Decoration cut or carved into clay, usually when the clay is leather-hard. The term implies a linear treatment, but often broad areas are so cut.

IRONSTONE—A dense, opaque white type of pottery.

JASPER—Unglazed, colored ware introduced by Wedgwood in 1776, characterized by white relief decoration over bodies of blue, green, lavender, or yellow.

LEATHER-HARD—A half-dry condition of pottery, sufficiently rigid to permit handling or carving, but still relatively moist.

LOW-FIRE, LOW-FIRED—Relative terms designating an approximate firing range, from the dull red heat of a bonfire to about pyrometric Cone 1, *c.* 2100 degrees F.

LUSTER—A minutely thin layer of metal over the surface of a glaze, similar in effect to the iridescent sheen of oil on water.

MAJOLICA—See FAIENCE. This term is often, perhaps erroneously, applied to opaque, shiny, colored glazes.

MAT, MATT, MATTE GLAZE—A glaze with a dull or nonshiny surface quality.

NONCRAZING, CRAZE-RESISTANT—Terms usually ascribed to functional pottery pertinent to ability to withstand use without crazing.

OPAQUE, OPACITY—Terms relative to the incapacity of materials to transmit light. A glaze is opaque if the clay body underneath is not apparent (although if freestanding, the same glaze would probably be translucent); an opaque body is non-translucent.

OVENWARE, OVENPROOF—Pottery cooking ware capable of being heated in the kitchen oven and removed without cracking.

PIN MARKS, SPUR MARKS, STILT MARKS—Blemishes left in the surface of a fired glaze after removal of supports used to hold the ware during glaze firing.

PORCELAIN—A vitreous, high-fired ware characterized by whiteness, translucency where thin, hardness, conchoidal (shell-like) fracture, and simultaneous firing of glaze and body.

REDUCING FIRE, REDUCTION—Kiln atmospheres in which there is insufficient oxygen to completely burn or oxidize the fuel, resulting in lower oxides of many coloring agents and in colors different from those of an oxidizing fire.

RESIST—A decorative technique in which areas of a body or a glaze are masked out with wax or rubber compounds, making them unreceptive to application of glaze or other decorative agents.

SALT GLAZE—A glaze produced by the introduction of salt into the incandescent kiln resulting in a deposit of a layer of glaze on the wares within the kiln.

SGRAFFITO—A decorative technique in which lines or areas are scratched or cut through a layer of slip or glaze, giving a pattern or decoration in the tonality of the underlying surface.

SHARD, SHERD—A pottery fragment.

SHIVERING—The flaking or chipping of a glaze from pottery following firing resulting from a greater contraction of body than glaze.

SINGLE-FIRED, ONCE-FIRED—Ware which has received its coating of glaze without an initial biscuit firing.

SLIP—Liquid clay.

SLIP DECORATION, SLIP PAINTING, SLIP TRAILING—Techniques by which pottery surfaces are decorated with liquid clays of colors differing from those of the body. Trailed decorations are accomplished with a device such as a tube, quill, or syringe, leaving a raised line; marbled or feathered effects, by moving slips of different colors while they are still fluid.

SLIP GLAZE—A glaze based on a low-melting, usually iron-bearing clay.

SOFT PASTE—A pottery type, usually white and translucent, which has glass or frit as its chief body flux, fired at a lower temperature than true or hard paste porcelain.

SPRIGGED, SPRIGGED-ON—A decorative technique in which clay ornaments are formed in molds before application to pottery surfaces.

STONEWARE—A broad category of pottery which includes wares which are quite dense or vitreous, opaque, off-white through tan, brown, and grey in color, and fired to a high degree.

TERRA SIGILLATA—A glossy pottery surface achieved by the application and sintering (partial fusion) of a layer of colloidal clay particles. The "glazes" of Greek pottery are coatings of this type rather than actual glassy fusions.

TIN ENAMEL—An opaque, white, shiny glaze containing tin oxide.

TRANSLUCENCY—The capacity of a material to transmit light but not a clear image. An attribute of thin porcelain, china, bone china, and many semi-opaque glazes.

TRANSPARENCY—The capacity of a material to transmit light without diffusion of visual image. An attribute of a clear sheet of glass and many glazes, but of no pottery bodies.

TURNED BASE OR FOOT—A base or foot of a pottery piece which has been shaped by removal of excess clay during the leather-hard stage.

UNDERGLAZE—Decorative pigments applied directly to a pottery body surface, usually covered by a transparent glaze.

VITREOUS—Glassy.

index

(Numbers refer to pages. Numbers in bold type indicate pages containing illustrations.)

adobe, 22
agate ware, 78
Albany slip clay, 11
alumina, 5
atmosphere, kiln, 27, 33, 93

Baggs, Arthur E., **16**, 36
ball clay, 9
basalt ware, 75
baskets, basketry, 74
Bauer, Fred, **69**
bodies, 14-20, 40
body color, 23, 91
bone china, 20, 23
bone-dry ware, 77
Böttger, Johann, 17
bright glazes, 90
burnished surfaces, 44, 45

calcined clay, 36
casting, 42-43
    slip, 42, 57
catenary arch kiln, **28**, 30
celadon glazes, 35, 94
ceramics, 1-3
chemically combined water, 41
china, 19
china clay, 6
clays, 6-11
cloisonné, **1**, 83
coil-building, 38, 44-45, **45**
coil-built pots, 74, **78**

color in bodies, 23, 91
color in glazes, 34, 92-94
colored slips, 78, 82
combed decoration, 79
common red clay, 10, 14, 24
conchoidal fracture, 16
cones (See pyrometric cones)
cooling, 33
copper glazes, 34, 36, 89, 93
copper red glazes, 34, 35, 93
Cornwall stone, 9
crackle glaze, **95**, 100
crystalline glaze, **91**
crystalline mat glazes, 90
cylindrical forms, 61, **61-64**

decoration, 74
deflocculants, 57
Delft ware, 14, 93
della Robbia, 59
drain casting, 42
draw trials, 32
Dunifon, Don, **71**

earthenware, **13**, 14
electric kilns, 27, **28**
electrolytes, 57
enamels, **1**, 1, 2, 3, 96, 98, **98**
    monochrome, **95**, 96
extrusion machine, 56

fabricative decoration, 75
faceted forms, **68-69**

factitious decoration, 75
feldspar, 5-7, 16, 23
Ferguson, Kenneth, **62**
fillers, 11
fireclay, 10
fire, firing, 21-25
firing cycles, 23-24
flux, 22, 89
fortuitous decoration, 75
fuels, 27, 33

Garzio, Angelo, **61, 67**
glass, 1, **2**, 89
glazes, 77, 78, 82, 88-94
   bright glazes, 90
   colored glazes, 92-93
   mat glazes, 90
   opaque glazes, 91
   salt glazes, 90
   slip glazes, 11, 24, 89, 90
   transparent glazes, 91
grain size, 7
granite, 5
grog, 11, 36
Grotell, Maija, **95**
Ground, John E., **71**

Hansen, Marc, **91**
Harder, Charles, 36
hard paste porcelain, 17
Hendry, Kenneth A., **71**
hump, throwing off, **52**

incised decoration, 79
insulating firebrick, 26
insulation, 26
iron in clays and bodies, 5, 11, 23, 75
iron in glazes, 34

jasper ware, 75, **81**
jiggering, 38, **53**

kaolin, 6, **8**, 9, 12, 41
   primary, 9
   secondary, 9
kaolinite, 6, 7
kaolinization, 7
kiln atmosphere, 27, 33, 93
kilns, 26-30, **28-29**
Klopfenstein wheel, **48**

Knoble, Joseph V., 46
Kottler, Howard, **62, 63, 68**

Leach, Bernard, **67**
Leach Pottery, The, **63**
leather-hard, 41, 51, 77
lids, **52**
Lin, Henry, **69**
Littlefield, Edgar, 36
local reduction, 36
luster, 15, 37, 77, 99

majolica, **63**, 94, 96, **97**, 99
Marx, Vaea, **71**
mat glazes, 90
McKinnell, James and Nan, **65**
Medici porcelain, 11, **20**
metals, 3, 96, 99
molds, 41-43, 79
monochrome enamels, 94, **95**
muffle kilns, **29**, 30
mullite, 16

neolithic ceramics, 44
nickel glaze colors, 35

opaque glazes, 91
organic materials, 11-12
ornament, 74
overglaze, 77
   decals, 96
   enamels, 77, 95, 96, 98
   painting, 96, 98
oxblood glazes, 34
oxidation, oxidizing fire, 33-35

Painter of London, **61**
particle size, 7, **8**
peach bloom glazes, 34
physically combined water, 41
Picasso, Pablo, **85**
pigeon blood glazes, 34
plaster of Paris, 41
plasticity in clay, 7, 41, 43
porcelain, 15, 16, 17, **18, 19**, 41, **95,
   97**
potter's wheel, 38, 43, 46, 47, **48**
pottery, 58
pouring spouts, **51, 52**
primary clays, 9

Pueblo pottery, 44, 46, **78, 85**
pyrometer, 30
Wedgwood, 32
pyrometric cones, **21**, 30-32, 37

raku, 25, 36
Randall wheel, **48**
reduction firing, 33-35, 36
refractory, 26-27
Reitz, Don, **70**
residual clays, 8
rib, throwing, 39, 40, **50**
Robineau, Adelaide Alsop, **18**
rutile colors, 35

saggars, 30
salt glaze, 83, **86**, 90
Schulman, Norman, **67**
secondary clays, 4, 8, 9
sedimentary clays, 9
Seger, Hermann, 32
sgraffito decoration, 82, **86, 87**
silica, 5, 89
slab construction, 54, **55**, 56
slip, 41
casting, 39, 41, 57
glazes, 11, 24, 89, 90
painting, 44, 77, 79, **84-87**
trailing, 83, **86**
soft paste porcelain, 17, **20**, 23
Soldner, Paul, 36, **63, 65, 66**

solid casting, 42
spherical forms, **65-67**
sprigged-on decoration, 79
Staffel, William, **19**
stoneware, 15
clays, 10

Takaezu, Toshiko, **70**
temper, 12
terra cotta, 10, 59
throwing, 39, 46-47, **49-50**
tin enamel, 91
titanium colors, 35
translucency, 16
transparent glazes, 91
treadle wheel, 47, **48**
tunnel kiln, **29**, 30
Turner, Robert, **62**

underglaze, underglaze painting, 77,
88, 96

vanadium colors, 35
Voulkos, Peter, **64**

weathering, 6-7
Wedgwood, Josiah, 32
pyrometer, 32
ware, 75, 79, **81**
Wyman, William, **68**

659